THE ISLAMIC CONQUESTS IN AFRICA

The Islamic Conquests In Africa

Swords of Faith

GEW Social Sciences Group

Hichem Karoui (Ed.)

Global East-West (London)

Copyright © 2024 by GEW Social Sciences Group
Hichem Karoui (Editor)
Global East-West (London)

All rights reserved. No part of this book may be reproduced in any manner whatsoever without written permission except in the case of brief quotations embodied in critical articles and reviews.

First Printing, 2024

CONTENTS

I - Prelude To Conquest 1

II - The Beginning: Egypt And North Africa . . . 13

References 24

III - Expansion Into The Maghreb 28

References 40

IV - The Conquest Of The Sudan 45

References 57

V - Eastward Expansion: The Horn Of Africa . . . 62

References 76

VI - Consolidation And Administration 78

References 90

VII - Legacy And Impact 94

References 107

VIII - The Military Strategies Of The Islamic Conquests 113

References 124

IX - The Role Of Key Figures In The Conquests . . 126

References 136

X - Reflections On The Islamic Conquests In Africa 138

I

PRELUDE TO CONQUEST

THE RISE OF ISLAMIC EMPIRES

Islam emerged as a powerful force in the Arabian Peninsula during the 7th century, marking the beginning of the rise of Islamic empires. With the advent of Islam and the teachings of the Prophet Muhammad, the people of Arabia experienced a transformative period that would ultimately shape the course of history. The unification of the Arabian tribes under the banner of Islam provided a sense of unity and purpose that transcended tribal loyalties, paving the way for establishing Islamic empires. The early Islamic empires, such as the Rashidun and Umayyad Caliphates, rapidly expanded their territories through military conquests and strategic alliances. The conquests in regions like Persia, Byzantium, and North Africa brought new lands and resources under Islamic rule, further solidifying the growing influence of Islam in the area. These conquests also facilitated the spread of Islamic teachings and practices, establishing Islam as a dominant cultural and religious force in the conquered territories. The rise of Islamic empires was not only a result of military conquests but also a reflection of the social, economic, and political changes that were taking place in the Arabian Peninsula. Establishing trade networks and developing urban centers created opportunities for economic prosperity and cultural exchange, strengthening the foundations of the Islamic empires.

Additionally, adopting administrative and legal structures helped govern the empires' diverse populations, ensuring stability and order. The rise of Islamic empires marked a period of significant cultural, intellectual, and scientific advancements. The translation of ancient Greek and Roman texts into Arabic, coupled with developments in fields such as mathematics, astronomy, and medicine, laid the groundwork for the flourishing of Islamic civilization. The Islamic empires also fostered a rich artistic and architectural tradition, creating magnificent mosques, palaces, and other structures showcasing Islamic culture's grandeur. In conclusion, the rise of Islamic empires in the Arabian Peninsula was a transformative period that reshaped the region's political, cultural, and religious landscape. The spread of Islam, the conquest of new territories, and the advancements in various fields contributed to the growth and influence of Islamic civilization, leaving a lasting legacy that continues to resonate today.

THE SPREAD OF ISLAM IN THE ARABIAN PENINSULA

The Arabian Peninsula, a region of vast deserts and nomadic tribes, witnessed a remarkable transformation with the spread of Islam. The rise of Islamic empires brought a new faith and a new way of life to the diverse peoples of the peninsula. This transformative process was challenging, as the early Muslim armies faced resistance and opposition from various factions. A combination of military conquests and peaceful conversions facilitated the spread of Islam in the Arabian Peninsula. The message of Islam resonated with many in the region with its monotheistic beliefs and emphasis on social justice. As Muslim armies advanced, they offered a choice to the conquered peoples: accept Islam and join the burgeoning Islamic community, or pay a tax and live under Muslim rule as protected subjects. The early Muslim armies employed a variety of tactics to achieve their conquests. They were skilled horsemen and expert archers, utilizing these abilities to affect the battlefield greatly. Their military strategies were marked by speed, flexibility, and coordination, allowing them to outmaneuver and outflank their adversaries. This agility was complemented by their use of siege engines and tactics, demonstrating a well-rounded and innovative approach to warfare. However, the spread of Islam in the Arabian Peninsula was not solely a military endeavor. The early Muslims also engaged in diplomatic efforts, forming alliances with local tribes and leaders to secure their positions and maintain regional stability. These alliances played a crucial role in expanding the reach of Islam and establishing a lasting presence in the peninsula. Overall, the spread of Islam in the Arabian Peninsula was a complex and multifaceted process, shaped by a combination of military conquests, diplomatic negotiations, and religious teachings. The early Muslim armies demonstrated remarkable skill and adaptability in their campaigns, paving the way for the emergence of a new civilization in the heart of the Arabian Peninsula.

THE MILITARY TACTICS OF THE EARLY MUSLIM ARMIES

The early Muslim armies employed several innovative military tactics that helped them achieve remarkable success in their conquests. One of the key strategies was the concept of mobility and flexibility on the battlefield. Unlike their opponents, the Muslim armies were highly mobile and could swiftly adapt to changing circumstances. They utilized their knowledge of the terrain to their advantage, often employing hit-and-run guerrilla tactics to harass and weaken their enemies before engaging them in more significant battles. This unpredictability kept their adversaries off-balance and gave the Muslim forces a considerable edge in combat. Another crucial aspect of their military tactics was decentralized command structures. Muslim commanders were given a high degree of autonomy and were empowered to make decisions based on the evolving situation on the battlefield. This flexibility allowed them to respond quickly to enemy movements and exploit any weaknesses they identified.

Moreover, the early Muslim armies were highly disciplined and well-trained, contributing to their combat effectiveness. They strictly adhered to their leaders' commands and followed rigorous training to ensure they were always prepared for battle. Furthermore, the Muslims utilized psychological warfare tactics to demoralize their opponents and sow fear among their ranks. They often employed psychological manipulation, deception, and propaganda tactics to weaken the enemy's resolve and create opportunities for victory. Overall, the military tactics of the early Muslim armies were characterized by their adaptability, mobility, discipline, and innovative approaches to warfare. These strategies played a crucial role in their conquests and laid the foundation for the expansion of the Islamic empire in the years to come.

THE EMERGENCE OF MUSLIM LEADERS

The emergence of Muslim leaders during the early Islamic period played a crucial role in shaping the expansion and success of the Muslim armies. These leaders, known for their strategic brilliance, courage, and devotion to the Islamic cause, were instrumental in guiding and uniting the diverse forces under their command. One prominent leader was Khalid ibn al-Walid, often called "the Sword of Allah." Known for his tactical genius and military prowess, Khalid was a key figure in several early Muslim conquests. His strategic maneuvers, quick decision-making, and ability to inspire his troops earned him a legendary reputation on the battlefield. Another notable leader was Amr ibn al-As, a skilled military commander who played a significant role in the conquest of Egypt. Amr's leadership abilities and diplomatic skills helped secure alliances and navigate complex political landscapes, leading to successful military campaigns in the region. These Muslim leaders rose to prominence for their military achievements and integrity, fairness, and commitment to justice. They upheld Islamic values of compassion, equality, and mercy, setting a high standard for governance in the newly conquered territories. As these leaders emerged and demonstrated their exceptional leadership qualities, they inspired and motivated their troops to persevere in the face of adversity and to achieve remarkable victories on the battlefield. Their legacy inspires admiration and respect, as their contributions to the early Islamic expansion are remembered and celebrated in the annals of history.

THE CROSSROADS OF CIVILIZATIONS: MECCA AND MEDINA

Nestled in the heart of the Arabian Peninsula, Mecca, and Medina are a testament to the rich tapestry of cultures and ideas that have converged in this region for centuries. These ancient cities served as vibrant hubs of trade, commerce, and cultural exchange, attracting merchants, pilgrims, and travelers from afar. With its sacred Kaaba at the center, Mecca held a special place in the hearts of the Arabs, serving as a focal point for religious rituals and ceremonies long before the advent of Islam. The annual pilgrimage, known as the Hajj, drew pilgrims from across the Arabian Peninsula, who came to pay homage to the idols housed in the Kaaba and participate in worship rituals. Medina, on the other hand, was a bustling oasis town known for its thriving marketplaces and diverse population. As a key stop on the trade routes connecting Arabia to the rest of the world, it was a melting pot of cultures and ideas, where merchants from as far as Syria and Persia mingled with the local population. With their rich history and vibrant communities, these two cities played a crucial role in shaping the early Islamic movement. The Prophet Muhammad's migration, or Hijra, from Mecca to Medina in 622 CE marked a turning point in the history of Islam, providing a haven for the fledgling Muslim community to grow and thrive. The significance of Mecca and Medina as centers of culture, trade, and religious devotion cannot be overstated. They served as the backdrop against which the early Muslim leaders emerged, forging alliances and laying the groundwork for the rapid expansion of Islam in the centuries to come.

THE CALL TO JIHAD: IDEOLOGICAL AND RELIGIOUS MOTIVATIONS

The Call to Jihad: Ideological and Religious Motivations The concept of jihad, often misunderstood in contemporary times, played a crucial role in the early Islamic conquests. Originating from the Arabic word "jihad," which means "struggle" or "striving," it encompassed both inner spiritual struggle and external physical struggle for the sake of Islam. For the early Muslim armies, the call to jihad served as a unifying force, rallying them behind a common cause and motivating them to fight for the expansion and preservation of the Islamic faith. Islamic teachings emphasized the importance of defending the community and spreading the message of Islam, which contributed to the fervor with which jihad was embraced. Moreover, the promise of rewards in the afterlife for those who died in battle, coupled with the belief in martyrdom as the ultimate sacrifice for the faith, further fueled the zeal of the Muslim warriors. They saw themselves as warriors of God, fighting not for personal gain but for the greater glory of Islam. Economic or political ambitions did not purely drive the early Islamic conquests but were deeply rooted in the religious and ideological fervor of the time. The call to jihad provided a sense of purpose and righteousness to the Muslim armies, guiding their actions and shaping the course of history in the process.

THE ROLE OF TRADE ROUTES IN FACILITATING EXPANSION

The Arabian Peninsula stood as a pivotal hub for trade and commerce at the crossroads of three continents. The bustling markets of Mecca and Medina attracted merchants from far and wide, creating a network of trade routes that crisscrossed the region. These trade routes facilitated the exchange of goods and served as conduits for the spread of ideas, cultures, and religions. The strategic location of the Arabian Peninsula allowed early Muslims to interact with diverse populations and cultures, leading to a cross-pollination of ideas and knowledge. As traders traveled along these routes, they carried not only goods but also the teachings of Islam. The message of the Prophet Muhammad spread through these trade networks, reaching distant lands and resonating with people from different backgrounds.

Furthermore, the wealth generated from trade provided the early Muslim community with resources to support their military campaigns. The profits from trade enabled the purchase of arms and supplies and the recruitment of soldiers to bolster the ranks of the expanding Muslim armies. Trade was a means of economic growth and a strategic asset in the conquests beyond Arabia. The interconnectedness of trade routes also allowed for alliances to be forged and diplomatic relations to be established with neighboring empires. The Abbasid Caliphate, for example, formed alliances with local rulers along trade routes, securing safe passage for their armies and ensuring the stability of newly conquered territories.

In conclusion, the role of trade routes in facilitating expansion cannot be understated. These networks not only propelled the economic growth of the early Muslim community but also served as conduits for the transmission of Islamic beliefs and practices. Trade was not merely a commercial endeavor but a vital component of the early Islamic conquests, shaping the geopolitical landscape of the time.

EARLY ENCOUNTERS WITH BYZANTINE AND PERSIAN EMPIRES

Even before the conquest of the Arabian Peninsula, the early Muslim armies found themselves in contact with the powerful Byzantine and Persian Empires. These encounters played a significant role in shaping the future trajectory of the Islamic conquests. The Byzantine Empire, centered in Constantinople, was a major power in the region. Its territories extended into the Levant, Egypt, and North Africa, presenting a formidable opponent to the emerging Muslim forces. On the other hand, the Persian Empire was based in Ctesiphon and exerted influence over the lands of Mesopotamia and beyond. The early Muslim encounters with these empires were characterized by conflict and negotiation. For example, the Battle of Mu'tah in 629 CE saw the Muslims facing off against Byzantine forces in the Levant. Although the battle resulted in a tactical retreat for the Muslims, it demonstrated their military capabilities and determination.

Similarly, interactions with the Persian Empire led to clashes, such as the Battle of the Bridge in 634 CE. These encounters showcased Muslim leaders' strategic understanding and ability to adapt to different military contexts. Despite initial setbacks, these early confrontations laid the groundwork for the later conquests of Byzantine and Persian territories. They provided valuable insights into the rival empires' strengths and weaknesses, informing the Muslim armies' military strategies in the subsequent campaigns. As the Islamic forces continued to expand their influence, the lessons learned from these early encounters with the Byzantine and Persian Empires would prove crucial in shaping the course of history in the region.

THE CONQUEST OF THE ARABIAN PENINSULA

The conquest of the Arabian Peninsula marked a significant turning point in the history of Islam, solidifying the nascent faith and establishing its dominance in the region. Led by the early Muslim armies, the conquests were characterized by military prowess, strategic alliances, and religious fervor. The key to the success of the conquests was the unity and discipline of the Muslim forces, which were inspired by the teachings of Islam and the promise of divine reward. Under the leadership of skilled commanders such as Khalid ibn al-Walid and Amr ibn al-As, the Muslim armies employed innovative tactics and strategies to overcome their adversaries. The internal divisions and weaknesses of the various tribes and city-states in the Arabian Peninsula also facilitated the conquests. The Muslim forces were able to exploit these divisions, forging alliances with some groups while confronting and subduing others. One of the most notable battles of the conquests was the Battle of Uhud, where the Muslims faced a significant defeat at the hands of the Quraysh tribe. Despite this setback, the Muslims regrouped and continued advancing, gradually consolidating their regional control. By the end of the conquests, the Arabian Peninsula was firmly under Muslim rule, paving the way for the further expansion of Islam into neighboring territories. The conquests not only secured the political and military dominance of the early Muslim community but also laid the foundations for establishing a new civilization based on the principles of Islam.

SETTING THE STAGE FOR CONQUESTS BEYOND ARABIA

With the conquest of the Arabian Peninsula solidified under the early Muslim leaders, the stage was now set for expansion beyond Arabia. The strategic location of Arabia at the crossroads of key trade routes and neighboring powerful empires served as a springboard for the Islamic forces to venture into new territories. The successful campaigns in Arabia demonstrated the Muslim armies' military prowess and showcased the religious and ideological fervor that motivated them. As the Muslim leaders consolidated their control over the Arabian Peninsula, they began to look outward towards new conquests. The rise of Islam and the expansion of the Muslim empire posed a direct challenge to the neighboring Byzantine and Persian empires, both weakened by years of conflict and internal strife. The emergence of a new political and religious power in the region threatened the existing power structures, creating a volatile environment ripe for further expansion. The teachings of Islam, emphasizing unity, community, and social justice, provided a mighty rallying cry for the Muslim armies as they marched toward new territories. The concept of jihad, or holy struggle, served as both a religious duty and a military strategy, inspiring the soldiers to fight with unwavering dedication and commitment. The vision of a unified Islamic empire under the banner of faith fueled the expansionist ambitions of the early Muslim leaders. As the Islamic empire expanded beyond Arabia, it encountered diverse cultures, religions, and peoples. The successful integration of these newly conquered territories into the growing Muslim empire required a delicate balance of military might, diplomacy, and administration. The development of new administrative and governance systems and the establishment of trade networks and cultural exchanges facilitated the assimilation of these diverse regions into the expanding Islamic civilization. The conquests beyond Arabia marked a turning point in the Islamic world's history, shaping the region's geopolitical landscape for centuries. The strategic victories achieved by the early Muslim leaders paved the way for further expansion and consolidation of the Islamic empire, setting the stage for the emergence of a new global power that would leave a lasting impact on world history.

II

THE BEGINNING: EGYPT AND NORTH AFRICA

THE REGION'S HISTORICAL SIGNIFICANCE

In the northeastern corner of Africa, Egypt holds a profound historical significance that stretches back thousands of years. Known as the "Gift of the Nile," Egypt's civilization emerged along the fertile banks of the Nile River, where the early Egyptians established one of the world's oldest and most enduring cultures. The ancient Egyptians were pioneers in various fields, including architecture, engineering, mathematics, art, and religion. They built awe-inspiring structures such as the pyramids and temples that continue to captivate and mystify people worldwide. Their sophisticated system of hieroglyphic writing and monumental works of art reflect a society rich in culture and tradition. Egypt's strategic location as a crossroads between Africa, the Middle East, and Europe made it a thriving trade and cultural exchange center. The wealth and resources of Egypt attracted the attention of various empires and civilizations throughout history, from the Greeks and

Romans to the Arabs and Ottomans. The legacy of ancient Egypt continues to resonate in the modern world, influencing art, architecture, and even popular culture. Understanding the historical significance of Egypt provides insight into the interconnectedness of civilizations and the enduring impact of one of humanity's earliest and most remarkable societies.

ANCIENT EGYPT: A LEGACY OF CIVILIZATION

Ancient Egypt stands as a monumental testament to the enduring legacy of civilization. With a history spanning over three millennia, the land of the Nile River holds a pivotal place in the annals of human history. The mighty pyramids, colossal statues, intricate hieroglyphs, and remarkable technological advancements all speak to the outstanding achievements of the ancient Egyptians. At the heart of Egyptian civilization was a complex social structure that witnessed the rise of powerful pharaohs revered as god-kings. These rulers oversaw the construction of magnificent structures such as the Great Pyramid of Giza, which still astounds visitors with its precision engineering and grandeur. The ancient Egyptians were pioneers in various fields, including architecture, engineering, medicine, and agriculture. Their advancements in irrigation techniques, such as the construction of the Nile dams and canals, enabled the sustainable cultivation of crops and facilitated the growth of a thriving agricultural economy.

Furthermore, the Egyptians made significant contributions to art and literature, with their intricate hieroglyphic writing system preserving their history and culture for future generations. The exquisite craftsmanship displayed in their artwork and the sophistication of their literary works continue to inspire awe and admiration. Religion was central to ancient Egyptian society, with a complex pantheon of gods and goddesses influencing every aspect of daily life. Temples dedicated to various deities served as worship centers and administrative hubs, underscoring ancient Egypt's close connection between religion and governance. In conclusion, the legacy of ancient Egypt reverberates through the corridors of time, reminding us of this illustrious civilization's remarkable achievements and enduring contributions.

ROMAN AND BYZANTINE INFLUENCE IN NORTH AFRICA

The Roman and Byzantine empires left indelible marks on the North African region through their extensive influence in various aspects of life. Their presence shaped the region's trajectory from governance and infrastructure to culture and religion for centuries. The Romans, known for their advanced engineering and architectural prowess, constructed impressive structures such as roads, aqueducts, and fortifications in North Africa. These infrastructural developments not only facilitated trade and communication but also served as a symbol of Roman authority and power in the region. Furthermore, the Romans introduced their legal and administrative systems, laying the foundation for North Africa's governance. With well-established institutions and regulations, the Roman presence brought a sense of order and stability to the region, reshaping local governance structures and practices. The Byzantine influence in North Africa, following the division of the Roman Empire, continued to impact the region significantly. The Byzantines brought with them Christianity, which gradually gained prominence and transformed the religious landscape of North Africa. Churches, monasteries, and other religious institutions emerged across the region, marking the spread of Christianity under Byzantine rule.

Moreover, the Byzantines extended their reach through trade and commerce, fostering economic growth and cultural exchange in North Africa. The integration of Byzantine trade networks with local markets boosted economic activity and facilitated the exchange of ideas and technologies, enriching the region's cultural tapestry. In conclusion, the Roman and Byzantine influence in North Africa was profound and enduring, shaping the region's development in various spheres. The legacy of their presence can still be observed in the architecture, governance structures, and religious traditions that continue to define the identity of North Africa today.

RISE OF CHRISTIANITY IN THE REGION

With its strategic location and rich cultural heritage, North Africa has long been a melting pot of different civilizations and religions. The rise of Christianity in the region marked a significant turning point in its history, shaping the religious landscape and influencing the sociopolitical dynamics of the time. The spread of Christianity in North Africa can be traced back to the early days of the Roman Empire when Christianity emerged as a distinct and growing faith within the diverse Roman society. The teachings of Jesus Christ resonated with many in the region, and over time, Christian communities began to form and expand across North Africa. One of the key figures in the early spread of Christianity in North Africa was Saint Augustine, a prominent theologian and philosopher born in present-day Algeria. Augustine's influential writings and teachings played a crucial role in shaping Christian theology and doctrine in the region, earning him a lasting legacy as one of the Church Fathers. The Christian communities in North Africa flourished under Roman and Byzantine rule, with churches and monasteries becoming centers of learning, piety, and community life. These Christian institutions played a vital role in preserving and transmitting knowledge and providing spiritual guidance and support to believers. However, the rise of Christianity in North Africa was not without challenges. The region witnessed periods of religious persecution and conflict as rival religious groups vied for dominance and political power. The dynamic interplay between Christian, pagan, and later Islamic influences contributed to a complex and multifaceted religious landscape in North Africa. Despite these challenges, Christianity continued to spread and thrive in North Africa, lasting and impacting the region's cultural, artistic, and intellectual development. The rich tapestry of Christian heritage in North Africa attests to the enduring legacy of this faith among the diverse peoples and communities of the region.

ARAB CONQUEST OF EGYPT IN THE 7TH CENTURY

The Arab conquest of Egypt in the 7th century marked a pivotal moment in the region's history. Led by the Islamic forces under the command of 'Amr ibn al-'As, the Arab armies swiftly advanced into Egypt in 639 CE. The conquest of Egypt was part of the larger Islamic expansion that aimed to spread the teachings of Islam and establish Muslim rule in new territories. The Byzantine Empire had previously controlled Egypt, but internal divisions and weakened defenses made it vulnerable to the Arab onslaught. The Arab forces, united by their faith and military prowess, quickly overcame the Byzantine defenses and captured major cities such as Alexandria and Memphis. The Arab conquest significantly changed Egypt's political, social, and religious landscape. While the region had a long history of Christianity, the arrival of Islam introduced a new monotheistic faith that would eventually become predominant. Despite initial resistance from the Coptic Christian population, many Egyptians embraced Islam and adopted Arabic as their primary language. Under Islamic rule, Egypt prospered as a center of trade, scholarship, and culture. The Arabs introduced new agricultural techniques, improved irrigation systems, and promoted economic development. The establishment of the city of Fustat (modern-day Cairo) as the capital of Egypt further solidified the region's importance within the Islamic world. The Arab conquest of Egypt not only transformed the region but also set the stage for spreading Islam across North Africa and beyond. The conquest served as a model for future Islamic expeditions and laid the foundation for the enduring influence of Islam in Egypt and the broader African continent.

ESTABLISHMENT OF ISLAMIC RULE IN NORTH AFRICA

After the Arab conquest of Egypt in the 7th century, establishing Islamic rule in North Africa brought significant changes to the region. The Islamic rulers implemented a new system of governance based on Islamic principles and laws. They established administrative structures to maintain law and order, promote justice, and enforce Islamic teachings. Under Islamic rule, North Africa saw a flourishing of art, architecture, and literature. Islamic scholars and intellectuals played a crucial role in preserving and advancing knowledge in various fields, such as medicine, astronomy, mathematics, and philosophy. The development of universities and libraries in major cities became learning centers, attracting scholars from across the Muslim world. Trade and commerce thrived under Islamic rule in North Africa. The region became a hub for exchanging goods, ideas, and cultures between Africa, Europe, and the Middle East. The construction of trade routes and ports facilitated the movement of goods and people, leading to economic growth and prosperity. Islamic rulers in North Africa also promoted agricultural development by introducing new irrigation techniques and crops. They invested in infrastructure projects such as roads, bridges, and water management systems to support agriculture and improve regional connectivity.

Furthermore, establishing Islamic rule in North Africa fostered a sense of unity among the region's diverse population. The spread of Islam brought people together under a common faith, transcending tribal and ethnic boundaries. Islamic values of brotherhood, equality, and community service contributed to social cohesion and stability in North Africa. The establishment of Islamic rule in North Africa during this period profoundly impacted the region's culture, economy, and society. It laid the foundation for a vibrant Islamic civilization that would flourish for centuries.

CULTURAL EXCHANGE AND ECONOMIC GROWTH

As Islamic rule was established in North Africa, a flourishing period of cultural exchange and economic growth ensued. Integrating Islamic traditions with local customs created a rich tapestry of artistic, architectural, and intellectual achievements. The development of trade networks facilitated the exchange of goods and ideas across the region and beyond, leading to economic prosperity. North African cities became essential hubs of commerce, attracting merchants and traders from diverse backgrounds. The Islamic Golden Age saw a vibrant cultural scene in North Africa, with scholars, poets, and artists contributing to the intellectual and artistic landscape of the region. Libraries and learning centers flourished, fostering a culture of inquiry and innovation. Fusing Islamic, Berber, and other local traditions created unique architectural styles, blending geometric designs, intricate tile work, and calligraphy. Mosques, palaces, and other structures showcased the era's artistic prowess and reflected North African society's cosmopolitan nature. During this period, economic growth and cultural exchange enhanced the region's prosperity and enriched its cultural heritage. The legacy of this era continues to resonate in the vibrant cities, diverse communities, and thriving artistic traditions of North Africa today.

CHALLENGES FACED BY EARLY MUSLIM RULERS

The early Muslim rulers in Egypt and North Africa faced many challenges as they sought to establish and maintain their regional rule. One of the primary obstacles they encountered was the existing power structures and opposition from the native populations. The transition from Byzantine and Roman rule to Islamic governance was not always smooth, and resistance from local elites and religious leaders posed a significant threat to the stability of the new regime. Moreover, the diversity of ethnic and cultural groups in the region presented a challenge for the early Muslim rulers. Managing the various interests and demands of different communities, including Arabs, Berbers, Copts, and others, required a delicate balance of power and diplomacy. The need to navigate these complex relationships while asserting authority and consolidating control over the territory tested the leadership and administrative skills of the early Muslim rulers.

Furthermore, economic stability and prosperity were essential for the success of the new Muslim administration. The management of resources, taxation, trade relations, and infrastructure development were crucial in ensuring the population's well-being and the state's viability. The early Muslim rulers faced the challenge of maintaining a delicate balance between extracting revenue for state coffers and ensuring the economic well-being of the people. In addition to these internal challenges, external threats and geopolitical tensions loomed large for the early Muslim rulers. The Byzantine Empire, the Berber tribes, and other neighboring powers posed constant challenges to the territorial integrity and security of the nascent Islamic state. Military campaigns, diplomatic maneuvering, and strategic alliances were essential tools in confronting these external threats and safeguarding the interests of the Muslim rulers. Overall, the early Muslim rulers faced challenges in Egypt and North Africa that were multifaceted and demanding. Navigating the complexities of governance, managing diverse populations, maintaining economic stability, and confronting external threats required strategic vision, political acumen, and resilience. The ability of the early Muslim rulers to confront and overcome these challenges would ultimately shape the course of Islamic history in the region.

INFLUENCE OF BERBER TRIBES IN THE REGION

The Berber tribes in North Africa played a significant role in the region's history and the spread of Islamic civilization. The Berbers were the area's indigenous people, with a longstanding history and unique cultural practices. As the early Muslim rulers established their presence in the region, they encountered the Berber tribes and sought to integrate them into the expanding Islamic empire. The Berbers were known for their strong sense of independence and warrior spirit, making them formidable allies or adversaries. Many Berber tribes initially resisted the Muslim conquest, leading to conflicts and challenges for the early Muslim rulers. However, over time, some Berber tribes embraced Islam and formed alliances with the Muslim conquerors, contributing to the consolidation of Islamic rule in North Africa. The influence of the Berber tribes in the region was profound, shaping the cultural, social, and political landscape of Egypt and North Africa. Their knowledge of the terrain and skills in warfare made them valuable assets for the Muslim rulers, aiding in the expansion and administration of the Islamic empire. The Berbers also brought their unique traditions, languages, and customs, enriching the region's diversity and contributing to developing a distinct Islamic civilization in North Africa. Through interactions with the Berber tribes, the early Muslim rulers learned to navigate the complexities of governing a diverse population and managing the territorial challenges of the region. The Berbers' resilience and adaptability played a crucial role in the success of the Islamic conquests and the establishment of lasting legacies in Egypt and North Africa. Their contributions to the region's history and the spread of Islamic civilization have left an indelible imprint on the cultural heritage of Egypt and North Africa.

LEGACY OF ISLAMIC CIVILIZATION IN EGYPT AND NORTH AFRICA

The legacy of Islamic civilization in Egypt and North Africa is profound and enduring. With the establishment of Islamic rule in the region, a new era of cultural exchange, economic growth, and intellectual development was ignited. The fusion of Arab, Berber, and other regional influences led to a rich and diverse Islamic civilization that left an indelible mark on the region's history. Architecture was one of the most significant contributions of Islamic civilization in Egypt and North Africa. The Arabs brought a sophisticated knowledge of engineering and design, which they used to construct mosques, palaces, and other grand structures that still testify to their skill and ingenuity. The iconic architecture of the region, characterized by intricate geometric patterns, elegant arches, and towering minarets, reflects the complex interplay of cultures and traditions that shaped Islamic civilization in the area. In addition to architecture, Islamic civilization in Egypt and North Africa made important advancements in science, medicine, and philosophy. Scholars and thinkers in the region translated and preserved ancient Greek and Roman texts, expanding the knowledge available to scholars and paving the way for future discoveries. The establishment of learning centers, such as the House of Wisdom in Baghdad, fostered a spirit of intellectual inquiry and innovation that attracted scholars from across the Islamic world. The legacy of Islamic civilization in Egypt and North Africa is also evident in the region's vibrant artistic traditions. From intricate calligraphy and decorative arts to vibrant textiles and ceramics, Islamic art in the region is characterized by its attention to detail, rich symbolism, and spiritual significance. Through their art, the people of Egypt and North Africa expressed their devotion to their faith and celebrated the beauty of the world around them.

Overall, the legacy of Islamic civilization in Egypt and North Africa is a testament to the enduring power of cultural exchange and intellectual curiosity. By embracing diverse influences and fostering innovation, the region's people created a vibrant and dynamic civilization that continues to inspire and captivate.

REFERENCES

Anastassiadou-Dumont, M. (2004). Bruce Masters, Christians and Jews in the Ottoman Arab world. The roots of sectarianism Cambridge, Cambridge University Press, «Cambridge studies in Islamic civilization,» 2001, 222 p. Annales: Histoire, Sciences Sociales, 59, 221–223.

Bat Yeʼor, The Decline of Eastern Christianity under Islam: From Jihad to Dhimmitude, Seventh–Twentieth Century, trans. Miriam Kochan and David Littman (Madison and Teaneck, N.J.: Fairleigh Dickinson University Press, 1996). Pp. 522.

Benabbès, Abderrezak. "Les premiers raids arabes en Numidie byzantine: questions toponymiques." In "Identités et cultures dans l'Algérie antique," 2005.

Bonté, 1984. Messaoudi, A. (2008). Savants, conseillers, médiateurs : les arabisants et la France coloniale (vers 1830-vers 1930).

Bonté, P. (1984). L'émirat de l'Adrar. Journal Des Africanistes, 54, 5–30.

Bostom, Andrew G. (ed.). "The Legacy of Jihad: Islamic Holy War and the Fate of Non-Muslims." Prometheus Books, 2005.

Bousquet, 1954- Charles-Roux, F. (1932). France et Afrique du Nord avant 1830 : les précurseurs de la conquête.

Bousquet, G. (1954). Les Élites Gouvernantes En Afrique Du Nord Depuis La Conquête Française1).

Butler, Alfred J. "The Arab Conquest of Egypt and the Last Thirty Years of the Roman Dominion." Oxford University Press, 1902 (reprinted 1978).

Chaker, 2008. Massignon, L. (1933). Histoire et Historiens de l'Algérie. Collection du Centenaire de l'Algérie. IV: Archéologie et Histoire. Journal of the Royal Asiatic Society, 65, 921-921.

Chaker, S. (2008). Libyque : écriture et langue. 4395–4409.

Charles-Roux, 1932. Ghilardi, M. (2014). La vallée du Nil en Haute-Égypte pendant la période dynastique : un exemple d'adaptation des sociétés humaines aux modifications hydrologiques dans le secteur de Karnak.

Charles-Roux, F. (1932). France et Afrique du Nord avant 1830 : les précurseurs de la conquête.

Chevallier, R. (1960). La paix romaine. Annales: Histoire, Sciences Sociales, 15, 793–799.

Chretien, J. (1985). Gwyn Prins, The Hidden Hippopotamus. Reappraisal in African History: the Early Colonial Expérience in Western Zambia, Cambridge, Cambridge University Press, 1980, xvi-319 p. Annales: Histoire, Sciences Sociales, 40, 1431–1434.

Clauss-Balty, P. (1999). Les Tombeaux en forme de tours en Afrique du Nord et au Proche-Orient aux époques héllenistique et romaine.

Coudray, C., Torroni, A., Achilli, A., Pala, M., Olivieri, A., Larrouy, G., & Dugoujon, J.-M. (2009). Les lignées mitochondriales et lhistoire génétique des populations berbérophones du nord de lAfrique. Anthropologie, 63–72.

Djait, H. (1973). L'Afrique arabe au VIIIe siècle (86-184 H./705-800). Annales: Histoire, Sciences Sociales, 28, 601–621.

Djaït, Hichem. "La conquête arabe de l'Afrique du Nord." Académie tunisienne des sciences, des lettres et des arts, 2007.

Donner, Fred M. "The Early Islamic Conquests." Princeton University Press, 1981.

Evans-Pritchard, E., August, T., & Idris, M. (1945). The Sanusi of Cyrenaica. Africa, 15, 61–79.

Fernández, V. M. (2011). Schematic Rock Art, Rain-Making and Islam in the Ethio-Sudanese Borderlands. African Archaeological Review, 28, 279–300.

Ghilardi, 2014. Clauss-Balty, P. (1999). Les Tombeaux en forme de tours en Afrique du Nord et au Proche-Orient aux époques héllenistique et romaine.

Ghilardi, M. (2014). La vallée du Nil en Haute-Égypte pendant la période dynastique : un exemple d'adaptation des sociétés humaines aux modifications hydrologiques dans le secteur de Karnak.

Gondonneau, A. (2001). Développement et application des techniques ICP-MS et LA-ICP-MS à la caractérisation de l'or: circulation monétaire entre Orient et Occident dans l'Antiquité et au Moyen-Age.

Gulbrandsen, Ø. (1993). The rise of the north-western Tswana kingdoms: on the dynamics of interaction between internal relations and external forces. Africa, 63, 550–582.

Hassab, S. (2009). L' évolution du fait urbain au Maroc du Nord: de la ville maurétano-romaine à la ville amazigho-islamique.

Hilali, A. (2013). Rome and Agriculture in Africa Proconsularis: Land and Hydraulic Development. Revue Belge De Philologie Et D Histoire, 91, 113–125.

Kaarsholm, P. (2011). TRANSNATIONAL ISLAM AND PUBLIC SPHERE DYNAMICS IN KWAZULU-NATAL: RETHINKING SOUTH AFRICA'S PLACE IN THE INDIAN OCEAN WORLD. Africa, 81, 108–131.

Kaegi, Walter E. "Muslim Expansion and Byzantine Collapse in North Africa." Cambridge University Press, 2010.

Kennedy, Hugh. "The Great Arab Conquests: How the Spread of Islam Changed the World We Live In." Da Capo Press, 2007.

Libyque: Écriture et Langue, 2008. Payraudeau, F. (2004). L'administration thébaine : la société et le pouvoir du début de la XXIIème dynastie jusqu'à la conquête éthiopienne.

Libyque: écriture et langue. (2008). 4395–4409.

Mahfoudh, Faouzi. "Les premiers siècles de l'Islam au Maghreb." Université de Tunis, 2015.

Marcus, I. (1994). Une communauté pieuse et le doute: mourir pour la Sanctification du Nom (Qiddouch ha-Chem) en Achkenaz (Europe du Nord) et l'histoire de rabbi Amnon de Mayence. Annales: Histoire, Sciences Sociales, 49, 1031–1047.

Massignon, L. (1933a). Histoire et Historiens de l'Algérie . Collection du Centenaire de l'Algérie. IV: Archéologie et Histoire. With an Introduction by Stéphane Gsell. By J. Alazard, etc. 9¼ × 7½, pp. 426. Paris: Félix Alcan, 1931. Frs. 60. Journal of the Royal Asiatic Society, 65, 921–921.

Mathien, 2007. Chevallier, R. (1960). La paix romaine. Annales. Histoire, Sciences Sociales, 15, 793-799.

Meadows, 2017. Djait, H. (1973). L'Afrique arabe au VIIIe siècle (86-184 H./705-800). Annales. Histoire, Sciences Sociales, 28, 601-621.

Messaoudi, A. (2008). Savants, conseillers, médiateurs: les arabisants et la France coloniale (vers 1830-vers 1930).

Modéran, Yves. "Les Maures et l'Afrique romaine (IVe-VIIe siècle)." École française de Rome, 2003.

Ohanna, N. (2009). Entre musulmanes, renegados e indios: narrativas españolas de convivencia en tierras extranjeras.

Payraudeau, F. (2004). L'administration thébaine: la société et le pouvoir du début de la XXIIème dynastie jusqu'à la conquête éthiopienne.

Ratti, S. (2005). L'Europe est-elle née dans l'Antiquité ? 193–211.

Robert, D. (1970). Les Fouilles De Tegdaoust. The Journal of African History, 11, 471–493.

Triaud, J. (1985). Le renversement du souverain injuste. Un débat sur les fondements de la légitimité islamique en Afrique noire au XIXe siècle. Annales: Histoire, Sciences Sociales, 40, 509–519.

Warscheid, I. (2021). The West African Jihād Movements and the Islamic Legal Literature of the Southwestern Sahara (1650–1850). Journal of West African History, 6, 33–60.

Zouanat, Z. (1989). Le pôle martyr Moulay´ Abd as-Salâm Ibn Machîch et son sanctuaire : étude historico-anthropologique.

III

EXPANSION INTO THE MAGHREB

INTRODUCTION TO THE MAGHREB REGION

The Maghreb, encompassing the northwestern corner of the African continent, holds a rich and diverse cultural tapestry woven over millennia. Known for its stunning landscapes, bustling marketplaces, and vibrant communities, this region has long been a crossroads of civilizations and trade routes. The Maghreb's strategic location, with its proximity to the Mediterranean Sea and its access to Europe and Africa, has shaped its history and fueled its growth. From the ancient Berber tribes that inhabited the land to the Phoenician and Roman influences that left their mark, the Maghreb has been a melting pot of cultures and traditions. As Islam began to spread across the Arabian Peninsula in the 7th century, it soon reached the shores of the Maghreb. The early Islamic presence in the region brought new religious and cultural practices that would eventually transform the landscape and shape the identity of its people. The Maghreb's diverse geography, ranging from the rugged Atlas Mountains to the vast Sahara Desert, presented challenges and opportunities for early Islamic settlers. The fertile coastal plains and river valleys provided fertile ground for agricultural development, while the arid interior posed challenges that required innovative solutions. Trade and commerce flourished in the Maghreb, with goods flowing between the Mediterranean world and the vast reaches of the African continent. Cities such as Tunis, Algiers, and Fez became vibrant centers of exchange and cultural exchange, attracting merchants, scholars, and travelers from far and wide. The Maghreb was a place of wonder and intrigue, from the bustling souks filled with exotic goods to the majestic mosques that dotted the skyline. East met West, and ancient traditions mingled with modern innovations. This introduction to the Maghreb region sets the stage for a deeper exploration of its history and significance in the context of the Islamic conquests.

EARLY ISLAMIC PRESENCE IN THE MAGHREB

The early Islamic presence in the Maghreb region dates back to the 7th century, following the Islamic Empire's rapid expansion under the Umayyad Caliphate's leadership. The conquest of North Africa by Muslim armies led to the establishment of Islamic rule in this strategic region, marking a significant shift in the cultural, political, and religious landscape of the Maghreb. The Islamic presence in the Maghreb was facilitated by the growing power and influence of the Arab tribes, who played a crucial role in spreading Islam beyond the Arabian Peninsula. The Arab conquerors brought with them their military prowess and religious fervor as they sought to propagate the teachings of Islam in the newly conquered territories. One of the key factors that contributed to the early Islamic presence in the Maghreb was the strategic importance of the region as a gateway to Europe and sub-Saharan Africa. The access to trade routes and resources made the Maghreb a coveted territory for various empires and civilizations throughout history. The spread of Islam in the Maghreb was not without resistance, as local Berber populations and other indigenous groups fiercely opposed the Arab conquest. However, cultural and religious assimilation took place over time, leading to the emergence of a distinct Islamic identity in the Maghreb region. The early Islamic presence in the Maghreb laid the foundation for a rich and diverse cultural heritage that continues to shape the identity of the region to this day. The legacy of the Islamic conquests is evident in the architecture, literature, music, and cuisine of the Maghreb, reflecting the enduring influence of Islam on the cultural landscape of North Africa.

FACTORS LEADING TO THE EXPANSION INTO THE MAGHREB

The factors that propelled the Islamic expansion into the Maghreb were multifaceted. One significant factor was the region's strategic location, which served as a gateway between North Africa and the rest of the Islamic world. The Maghreb's proximity to key trade routes and its access to the Mediterranean Sea made it a vital area for economic and commercial activities. Additionally, the political landscape of the Maghreb at the time provided an opportunity for Islamic expansion. The region was characterized by fragmented Berber tribes and weakened Byzantine and Roman influence, creating a power vacuum that Islamic forces sought to fill. The decentralized nature of the Maghreb made it ripe for conquest and consolidation under a unified Islamic authority. Religious motivations also played a crucial role in the expansion into the Maghreb. The spread of Islam was not only viewed as a religious duty but also as a means to establish a more cohesive and centralized Islamic state. By converting the indigenous populations to Islam, the conquerors sought to create a sense of unity and common identity among the diverse inhabitants of the Maghreb.

Moreover, the allure of wealth and resources in the Maghreb incentivized Islamic powers to expand into the region. The fertile lands, abundant natural resources, and thriving trade networks presented economic opportunities that motivated Islamic forces to seek control over the Maghreb. The extraction of wealth from the region also contributed to the expansionist ambitions of Islamic rulers. The internal dynamics of the Islamic world, including political rivalries and ambitions for territorial expansion, further fueled the drive to conquer the Maghreb. Islamic empires sought to extend their influence and establish dominance over the region as part of broader imperial ambitions. The conquest of the Maghreb was a strategic military objective and a demonstration of power and authority in the Islamic world.

KEY EVENTS AND BATTLES IN THE CONQUEST OF THE MAGHREB

The Islamic Conquest of the Maghreb was marked by key events and pivotal battles that shaped the course of history in the region. One such significant event was the Battle of Walaja, where the Arab forces led by Khalid ibn al-Walid clashed with the Sassanid Empire, resulting in a decisive victory for the Muslims. Another crucial battle was the Battle of Yarmouk, where the Rashidun Caliphate's army, under the command of Khalid ibn al-Walid, faced the Byzantine Empire's forces. The Muslim army's strategic brilliance and military prowess led to a resounding victory, paving the way for the conquest of the Levant and, eventually, the Maghreb. The conquest of Egypt by the Arab forces was a turning point in the expansion into the Maghreb. The Battle of Nikiou, where the Arabs defeated the Byzantine forces, opened the door for further advances westward. Subsequent battles in North Africa, such as the Battle of Sufetula, saw the Muslim armies overcoming fierce resistance and consolidating their control over the region. The siege of Carthage, a key stronghold in North Africa, proved to be a critical juncture in the conquest of the Maghreb. The fall of Carthage to the Muslim forces marked the end of Byzantine rule in the region and solidified Islamic dominance. Overall, the conquest of the Maghreb was a complex series of events marked by strategic battles and military campaigns that reshaped the political and cultural landscape of the region. The legacy of these conquests continues to endure in the Maghreb's history and heritage.

RESISTANCE AND OPPOSITION FROM INDIGENOUS POPULATIONS

The Islamic conquest of the Maghreb was not without its challenges, as indigenous populations in the region often put up fierce resistance to the invading forces. The Berber tribes, in particular, fiercely defended their lands and way of life against the advancing armies of the Islamic caliphate. The mountainous terrain of the Maghreb provided a natural advantage to the Berber fighters, who were skilled in guerrilla warfare tactics. They used hit-and-run tactics, ambushing Islamic forces and then retreating into the rugged landscape, making it difficult for the invaders to pursue them effectively. The Berbers were also united by a strong sense of identity and shared culture, providing them with a powerful sense of unity in the face of external threats. This cohesion allowed them to coordinate their resistance efforts and mount effective campaigns against the Islamic forces. Despite facing superior military technology and disciplined armies, the Berbers' intimate knowledge of the land and fierce determination to resist foreign occupation made them formidable foes. The Islamic conquerors were often surprised by the tenacity and resilience of the indigenous populations they encountered in the Maghreb. The resistance by the Berber tribes not only slowed the pace of the Islamic conquest but also forced the invaders to adopt different strategies to subdue the local populations. Diplomatic negotiations, alliances with certain tribal factions, and establishing garrisons in key strategic locations were some methods used to pacify the resistant Berber groups. The clashes between the Berber resistance fighters and the Islamic armies were marked by brutality and bloodshed on both sides. The struggle for control of the Maghreb was not just a military campaign but a clash of cultures, ideologies, and identities that would shape the region's history for centuries to come.

ADMINISTRATION AND GOVERNANCE OF THE CONQUERED TERRITORIES

The administration and governance of the conquered territories in the Maghreb region were crucial aspects of the Islamic conquests. After overcoming resistance from indigenous populations, the Islamic rulers established systems to maintain control and stability in the newly acquired lands. The governance structure was characterized by appointing governors or emirs to oversee different regions. These governors were responsible for implementing Islamic law, known as Sharia, and ensuring compliance with the new social and political order. They also oversaw the collection of taxes and the distribution of resources to support the ruling authority. One key aspect of the administration was the integration of existing administrative structures with Islamic governing principles. Local officials were often retained to help facilitate the transition and maintain order among the population. This approach helped minimize disruptions and foster a sense of continuity for the conquered territories.

Furthermore, the Islamic rulers implemented policies to promote economic development and infrastructure improvement in the conquered territories. They encouraged trade and commerce, built mosques and schools, and established learning centers to promote Islamic culture and education. This comprehensive approach to governance aimed to foster a sense of unity and stability in the region. In addition to political and economic governance, the Islamic conquerors also focused on cultural and religious administration. They respected the spiritual practices of the indigenous populations and often allowed them to continue worshiping their deities alongside the Islamic faith. This religious tolerance policy helped maintain social harmony and prevent widespread unrest. Overall, the administration and governance of the conquered territories in the Maghreb region played a crucial role in shaping the legacy of the Islamic conquests. By implementing effective rule systems, the Islamic rulers could consolidate their power, promote cultural exchange, and establish a lasting influence on the region.

CULTURAL AND RELIGIOUS IMPACT OF THE ISLAMIC CONQUEST IN THE MAGHREB

The Islamic conquest of the Maghreb region had a profound cultural and religious impact that reshaped the societal fabric of the area. As Islamic rule extended into the Maghreb, a new set of religious beliefs, practices, and cultural norms began influencing the local populations. One of the key aspects of the cultural impact of the Islamic conquest was the spread of Arabic language and script. Arabic became the newly conquered territories' administration, education, and religious language. Islamic scholars and teachers from the Arab heartlands disseminated knowledge and learning, ensuring that Arabic became a linguistic, cultural, and intellectual medium in the Maghreb. The arrival of Islam also introduced new architectural styles, as mosques, madrasas, and palaces were built in the Islamic architectural tradition, adorned with intricate geometric patterns and calligraphic inscriptions. These structures served as places of worship and learning and as symbols of Islamic cultural and religious dominance in the region.

Moreover, the Islamic conquest facilitated the spread of Islamic art and music, influencing local artistic traditions and aesthetics. Calligraphy, geometric designs, and arabesques became prominent features of Maghrebi art, reflecting the fusion of indigenous artistic practices with Islamic influences. Religiously, the Islamic conquest led to the conversion of many indigenous peoples to Islam. The spread of Islamic beliefs and practices throughout the Maghreb region forged a common religious identity among diverse ethnic and tribal groups. Islamic festivals, rituals, and moral codes became integral parts of daily life, shaping the social and ethical values of the populace.

Furthermore, the integration of Islamic legal principles and governance systems brought a sense of unity and cohesion to the conquered territories. Establishing Sharia law and promoting Islamic jurisprudence helped establish a common legal framework transcending previous tribal and ethnic divisions. Overall, the cultural and religious impact of the Islamic conquest in the Maghreb was far-reaching, transforming the region's cultural landscape and shaping its identity for centuries to come.

TRADE AND ECONOMIC INTEGRATION IN THE MAGHREB REGION

In the wake of the Islamic conquest of the Maghreb region, a new era of trade and economic integration blossomed, transforming the socio-economic landscape of the territories. The strategic location of the Maghreb served as a gateway between the Mediterranean Sea and the Sahara Desert, facilitating trade routes that connected North Africa with Europe, the Middle East, and sub-Saharan Africa. The Islamic conquerors recognized the region's economic potential and sought to capitalize on its resources and trading opportunities. Major cities such as Kairouan, Fez, and Tunis emerged as vibrant commercial hubs where goods from different regions were exchanged, creating a bustling marketplace that attracted traders from far and wide. Under Islamic rule, the Maghreb experienced an influx of merchants and traders who brought various products, including spices, textiles, ceramics, and precious metals. This exchange of goods enriched the local economy and fostered cultural exchange and cross-cultural interactions among diverse populations.

Furthermore, the Islamic conquerors implemented policies to promote economic growth and stability in the region. They established centers for crafts and industries, supported agricultural development, and improved infrastructure such as roads and bridges to facilitate trade and commerce. Integrating the Maghreb into the wider Islamic world brought new economic opportunities through increased access to markets and technologies. Adopting Arabic as the language of administration and commerce further facilitated trade relations with other Islamic regions, enhancing economic cooperation and exchange. Despite the economic prosperity and trade networks that flourished in the Maghreb, the region faced challenges in maintaining control and stability. Competition among local rulers, conflicts over trade routes, and external threats from rival powers posed significant obstacles to the region's economic integration. In navigating these challenges, the Islamic rulers of the Maghreb demonstrated diplomatic skill and political acumen, forging alliances with local tribes and neighboring empires to safeguard trade routes and ensure the uninterrupted flow of goods across the region. Overall, the trade and economic integration of the Maghreb region during the Islamic conquests played a pivotal role in shaping its development and connecting it to the broader networks of the Islamic world. This era of economic prosperity and exchange left a lasting legacy that continues to influence the socio-economic dynamics of the region to this day.

CHALLENGES FACED IN MAINTAINING CONTROL AND STABILITY

The Islamic conquest of the Maghreb region presented several challenges in maintaining control and stability. One of the primary difficulties faced by the conquering forces was the vastness of the territory and the diverse nature of the local populations. The Maghreb encompassed various ethnic groups with customs, languages, and social structures. This diversity made it challenging to enforce centralized control and ensure loyalty to the new Islamic rulers. Furthermore, the rugged terrain of the Maghreb, which included mountain ranges, deserts, and coastal regions, posed logistical challenges for the governing authorities. Maintaining communication and transportation networks across such varied landscapes was a complex task, leading to difficulties in quickly responding to threats or uprisings. Another significant challenge was the presence of pockets of resistance from indigenous populations who were opposed to the Islamic conquest. Some tribes and communities in the Maghreb fiercely resisted the new rulers, often engaging in guerrilla warfare and launching surprise attacks on Islamic garrisons. This resistance prolonged the pacification and integration of the region into the Islamic caliphate.

Additionally, the economic challenges of the Maghreb presented obstacles to maintaining stability. The region was known for its trade routes and financial resources, but controlling and regulating commerce required effective governance and infrastructure. Competition among various factions for control over lucrative trade routes and resources sometimes led to regional conflicts and instability. Overall, the challenges faced in maintaining control and stability after the Islamic conquest of the Maghreb underscored the complexities of governing a diverse and vast territory. It required tact, diplomacy, and strategic planning to navigate the region's intricate social, political, and economic landscape and secure long-term stability under Islamic rule.

LEGACY OF THE ISLAMIC CONQUEST IN THE MAGHREB

The Islamic conquest of the Maghreb left a profound and lasting legacy on the region. One of the most significant impacts was the spread of Islam, which became a dominant religion in the Maghreb and profoundly influenced the inhabitants' culture, customs, and way of life. The Islamic conquest also introduced new systems of governance and administration, laying the foundation for the development of organized states in the region. The establishment of Islamic law and institutions helped create a sense of unity among the diverse populations of the Maghreb. Furthermore, integrating the Maghreb into the wider Islamic world facilitated the exchange of ideas, knowledge, and technologies, leading to advancements in various fields such as architecture, science, and literature. This cultural exchange enriched the fabric of Maghrebi society and contributed to its development. The Islamic conquest of the Maghreb also had a lasting impact on trade and economic integration in the region. The establishment of trade routes and networks connecting the Maghreb to other parts of the Islamic world stimulated economic growth and prosperity, fostering commercial activities and the exchange of goods and resources. Despite facing challenges in maintaining control and stability in the region, the Islamic conquest left a legacy of cultural, economic, and political transformation that shaped the identity of the Maghreb and continues to influence its trajectory to this day.

REFERENCES

Arabic:

1. 1996. ابن عبد الحكم، عبد الرحمن. "فتوح مصر والمغرب." دار الفكر.
2. 1988. البلاذري، أحمد بن يحيى. "فتوح البلدان." دار ومكتبة الهلال.
3. 1995. الطالبي، محمد. "الدولة الأغلبية." دار الغرب الإسلامي.
4. 2000. حسين مؤنس. "فتح العرب للمغرب." مكتبة الثقافة الدينية.
5. عبد العزيز سالم. "تاريخ المغرب في العصر الإسلامي." مؤسسة شباب الجامعة، 1982.
6. مغزاوي مصطفى (2013). "التطور العقيدي في المغرب الإسلامي من الفتح إلى نهاية القرن العاشر هجري.
7. موسى, ع. ا., & الكحلاوي, م. (2020). أضرحة مدينة ولاته الموريتانية دراسة تاريخية حضارية Walata Mausoleum in Mauritania An Historical and Civilization Study. 22, 520–548.

English:

1. Kennedy, Hugh. "The Great Arab Conquests: How the Spread of Islam Changed the World We Live In." Da Capo Press, 2007.
2. Abun-Nasr, Jamil M. "A History of the Maghrib in the Islamic Period." Cambridge University Press, 1987.
3. Bennison, Amira K. "The Great Caliphs: The Golden Age of the 'Abbasid Empire." Yale University Press, 2009.
4. Hrbek, Ivan (ed.). "General History of Africa III: Africa from the Seventh to the Eleventh Century." UNESCO, 1992.
5. Savage, Elizabeth. "A Gateway to Hell, a Gateway to Paradise: The North African Response to the Arab Conquest." Darwin Press, 1997.
6. Djelaili, Ahmed (2020). "A NEW READING OF HISTORICAL ACCOUNTS ABOUT THE RULE OF THE BARBARIAN QUEEN (ELKAHINA) AND HER RESISTANCE TO THE ISLAMIC ARMY OF CONQUEST LED BY HASSAN IBN AL-NUMAN (39-74 A.H./658-693 CE)".

7. Toral, I. (2022). "The Umayyad Dynasty and the Western Maghreb. A Transregional Perspective". Medieval Worlds.

8. Lourinho, Inês (2022). "Military Jihād against Muslims: 'Abd Allāh b. Yāsīn and the Foundation of a Saharan Political Unit that Would Conquer the Maghreb and al-Andalus (Eleventh Century)." Al-Masāq, 35, 119-142.

9. Stepanova, A. (2018). "Who Conquered Spain? The Role of the Berbers in the Conquest of the Iberian Peninsula". Written Monuments of the Orient.

French:

1. Laroui, Abdallah. "L'Histoire du Maghreb: Un essai de synthèse." Centre Culturel Arabe, 2001.

2. Djait, Hichem. "La conquête arabe de l'Afrique du Nord et la résistance berbère." Les Éditions de Minuit, 2004.

3. Djait, H. (1973). "L'Afrique arabe au VIIIe siècle (86-184 H./705-800)". Annales. Histoire, Sciences Sociales, 28, 601-621.

4. Messaoudi, A. (2008). "Savants, conseillers, médiateurs : les arabisants et la France coloniale (vers 1830-vers 1930)".

5. Modéran, Yves. "Les Maures et l'Afrique romaine (IVe-VIIe siècle)." École Française de Rome, 2003.

6. Siraj, Ahmed. "L'Image de la Tingitane: L'historiographie arabe médiévale et l'Antiquité nord-africaine." École Française de Rome, 1995.

7. Talbi, Mohamed. "L'Émirat aghlabide, 184-296/800-909: Histoire politique." Adrien Maisonneuve, 1966.

Further Research

Amara, A. (2016). Ifriqiya, medieval empires of (Aghlabid to Hafsid). 1–13.

BADI, O. M., & Reda, R. (2023). EDUCATION IN ISLAMIC MAGHREB DURING THE MIDDLE AGE BETWEEN IBN SAHNOUN AND IBN KHALDOUN. RIMAK International Journal of Humanities and Social Sciences.

Burshatin, I. (2017). Narratives of the Islamic conquest from medieval Spain. Modern Language Review, 18, 213–214.

Djelaili, A. (2020). A NEW READING OF HISTORICAL ACCOUNTS ABOUT THE RULE OF THE BARBARIAN QUEEN (ELKAHINA) AND HER

RESISTANCE TO THE ISLAMIC ARMY OF CONQUEST LED BY HASSAN IBN AL-NUMAN (39-74 A.H./658-693 CE). 2, 01–18.

Fentress, E. (2022). Islamizing Berber Lifestyles. Medieval Worlds.

Fournier, E. J. (2016). Christianity in Roman Africa: The Development of Its Practices and Beliefs by J. Patout Burns and Robin M. Jensen (review). The Catholic Historical Review, 102, 132–133.

García-Sanjuán, A. (2019). Denying the Islamic conquest of Iberia: A historiographical fraud. What Was the Islamic Conquest of Iberia?, 11, 306–322.

Gasc, S. (2019). Numismatics data about the Islamic conquest of the Iberian Peninsula. What Was the Islamic Conquest of Iberia?, 11, 342–358.

Hazbun, G. (2014). Narratives of the Islamic Conquest from Medieval Spain.

Jackson, P. (2017). The Mongols and the Islamic World: From Conquest to Conversion.

Kadhim, M. S. (2022). Historiography in al-Andalus "The Historian Abd al-Malek Andalusi as Model." Uluslararası Prof. Dr. Halil İnalcık Tarih ve Tarihçilik Sempozyumu Bildiriler II. Cilt.

Khudair, L. A., & Al-Samarrai, P. D. O. A. H. (2022). Feasts and occasions in Morocco in the era of rulers. International Journal of Research in Social Sciences and Humanities.

Lajlaj, Ass. P. Dr. A. A.-K. (2022). Attempts to dispel the efforts of the Arab Islamic conquest of Andalusia between conspiracy and deception "92-95 AH" a critical analytical study. Thi Qar Arts Journal.

Lenfest, Y. (2022). Khaled El-Rouayheb's Islamic Intellectual History in the Seventeenth Century: Scholarly Currents in the Ottoman Empire and the Maghreb. Journal of Islamic Philosophy.

Lines, J., & Ghirshman, R. (1955). Iran: From the Earliest Times to the Islamic Conquest. American Journal of Archaeology, 59, 332.

May, T. (2021). The Mongols and the Islamic World: From Conquest to Conversion. By Peter Jackson. Journal of the American Oriental Society.

Mazzola, M. (2024). Diplomats and Betrayers: Christian Negotiators and the Confessional Rewriting of Surrender during the Islamic Conquest (634–642 AD). Al-Masaq, 36, 78–104.

Milanovic, B. (2013). Income Level and Income Inequality in the Euro-Mediterranean Region: From the Principate to the Islamic Conquest. Economic History eJournal.

Mirza, G. A. (2021). Specialties and Medical Services in Andalusia From the Islamic Conquest to the Era of the Kings of the Taifas (92 AH - 422 AH / 711 AD - 1031 AD). Journal of University of Raparin.

Park, H. (2023). The Position of the Maghreb in Traditional Chinese Geographical Knowledge about the Islamic Middle East. Maghreb Review, 38, 20–23.

Peterson, D. (2020a). Quintana place-names as evidence of the Islamic conquest of Iberia. Journal of Medieval Iberian Studies, 12, 155–176.

Peterson, D. (2020b). The Languages of the Invaders of 711, Invasion and Language Contact in Eighth–Century Northwestern Iberia*. 59, 527–535.

Ramírez-Río, J. (2012). Al-Ḏajīra al-saniyya: una fuente relevante para el siglo XIII en la Península Ibérica.

Raymond, A. (2002). Arab Cities in the Ottoman Period: Cairo, Syria and the Maghreb.

Sanjuán, A. G. (2018). La creciente difusión de un fraude historiográfico: la negación de la conquista musulmana de la península ibérica Denying the Islamic conquest of Iberia, an increasingly prevalent historiographical fraud. 173–193.

Schriber, A. (2022). Jocelyn Hendrickson, Leaving Iberia: Islamic Law and Christian Conquest in North West Africa. Islamic Law and Society.

Scott Savran. Arabs and Iranians in the Islamic Conquest Narrative: Memory and Identity Construction in Islamic Historiography, 750–1050 (New York: Routledge, 2018). Pp. 248.

Shatzmiller, M. (2000). The Berbers and the Islamic state: the Marīnid experience in pre-protectorate Morocco.

Staëvel, J.-P. V. (2023). Ribât in Early Islamic Ifrîqiya: Another Islam from the Edge. Religions.

Stepanova, A. (2018). Who Conquered Spain? The Role of the Berbers in the Conquest of the Iberian Peninsula. Written Monuments of the Orient.

Thalal, A., Aboufadil, Y., Raghni, M. A. E., Jali, A., Oueriagli, A., & Rai, K. A. (2017). Symmetry in art and architecture of the Western Islamic world. Crystallography Reviews, 24, 102–130.

THE ISLAMIC CONQUEST: (2021). The Christian Communities of Palestine_x000B_from Byzantine to Islamic Rule.

Toral, I. (2022). The Umayyad Dynasty and the Western Maghreb. A Transregional Perspective. Medieval Worlds.

Vernet, A. (2023). Dwelling Transformation and Evolution of Customs after the Islamic Conquest in Near Eastern Cities.

Warscheid, I. (2017). The Persisting Spectre of Cultural Decline: Historiographical Approaches to Muslim Scholarship in the Early Modern Maghreb. Journal of The Economic and Social History of The Orient, 60, 142–173.

Zakrzewski, S. (2015). Religious disruption and the Islamic conquest of Andalucia.

IV

THE CONQUEST OF THE SUDAN

THE SUDAN REGION

The Sudan region in northeast Africa is a land shrouded in mystery and rich history. Stretching from the Nile River to the Red Sea, this vast expanse of land has been home to various civilizations and cultures that have left their mark on the landscape. The Sudan region is known for its unique geography, with the Nile River serving as the area's lifeblood. The fertile banks of the Nile have supported thriving agricultural communities for centuries, while the surrounding deserts have posed challenges to those seeking to traverse the region. In ancient times, the Sudan region was home to several powerful kingdoms and empires, such as the Kingdom of Kush and the Kingdom of Meroe. These civilizations rose and fell, leaving behind impressive ruins and artifacts that provide clues to their sophisticated societies. The people of the Sudan region have a rich cultural heritage, with traditions passed down through generations. From intricate artwork to vibrant music and dance, the Sudan region is a melting pot of diverse influences that have blended together to create a unique and dynamic cultural tapestry. As we delve deeper into the history of the Sudan region, we will uncover the fascinating stories of the civilizations that once thrived here and explore how these ancient cultures continue to shape the identity of this vibrant region today.

PRE-ISLAMIC SUDAN: CIVILIZATIONS AND CULTURES

The Sudan region in Northeast Africa boasts a rich history of civilizations and cultures dating back to ancient times. Before the spread of Islam into the region, pre-Islamic Sudan was home to several diverse societies that thrived along the Nile River and its surrounding areas. One of the earliest known civilizations in the Sudan region was the Kingdom of Kush, which flourished from around 1070 BC to 350 AD. The Kingdom of Kush was a powerful empire controlling vast territories and trading with neighboring cultures. Known for their impressive architecture, including the pyramids at Meroe, the Kushites left a lasting legacy on the region. Another significant civilization of pre-Islamic Sudan was the Kingdom of Aksum, located in present-day Ethiopia and Eritrea. The Aksumites were known for their advanced trade networks and being one of the first civilizations to adopt Christianity in the region. Their influence extended into the Sudan region, shaping the cultural and religious landscape. The Nubian civilization, centered around the city of Napata, also played a crucial role in shaping pre-Islamic Sudan. Known for their skilled craftsmanship and distinctive pottery, the Nubians maintained close ties with neighboring societies and engaged in trade across the region. In addition to these major civilizations, the Sudan region was home to a variety of smaller tribes and societies that contributed to the cultural tapestry of the area. These diverse groups engaged in agriculture, trade, and artistic expression, creating Sudan's dynamic and vibrant pre-Islamic society. Overall, the civilizations and cultures of pre-Islamic Sudan laid the foundation for the region's future development and played a pivotal role in shaping its identity. The legacy of these early societies can still be seen in modern-day Sudan's traditions, art, and architecture, highlighting the enduring impact of their contributions.

THE SPREAD OF ISLAM INTO SUDAN

The spread of Islam into Sudan was a significant journey marked by cultural and historical transformations. As Islam began to gain momentum in the neighboring regions, it eventually made its way into the diverse lands of Sudan. Islamization in Sudan was not a sudden occurrence but a gradual integration over several centuries. Trade routes were crucial in facilitating the exchange of goods, ideas, and religious beliefs between Sudan and the wider Islamic world. Merchants and travelers traversed the desert terrain, bringing with them the teachings of Islam and introducing them to the local populations. This exchange of goods and ideas created a fertile ground for introducing and accepting Islam among the people of Sudan. The spread of Islam into Sudan was also influenced by the migration of Muslim communities southward from Egypt and the Arab world. These communities settled in various parts of Sudan, establishing centers of Islamic learning, trade, and religious practice. Over time, these settlements grew into vibrant urban centers that became hubs of Islamic scholarship and cultural exchange. As Islam continued to take root in Sudan, it began to intersect with the region's existing indigenous beliefs and traditions. This fusion of Islamic teachings with local customs and practices laid the foundation for a unique Sudanese Islamic identity that continues to shape the region's cultural landscape to this day. The adoption of Islam in Sudan was not without its challenges and resistance. Some communities resisted the spread of Islam, clinging to their traditional beliefs and practices. However, through a combination of diplomacy, trade, and cultural exchange, Islam gradually gained acceptance and prominence in Sudan, eventually becoming the dominant faith of the region. In conclusion, the spread of Islam into Sudan was a multifaceted process that unfolded over time, blending elements of trade, migration, and cultural exchange. This transformation not only reshaped the religious landscape of Sudan but also influenced its social, political, and economic structures, leaving a lasting imprint on the region's history.

INITIAL ISLAMIC INCURSIONS INTO SUDAN

A gradual and strategic expansion of influence and power characterized the initial Islamic incursions into the Sudan region. In the early days of Islam's spread into the region, Arab traders and travelers played a significant role in introducing the religion and fostering diplomatic relations with local tribal leaders and rulers. These initial interactions laid the foundation for future military campaigns and conquests. The first incursions into Sudan were not large-scale military invasions but rather focused on establishing trade networks and diplomatic ties and spreading the message of Islam. Arab merchants utilized the existing trade routes in the region to establish economic connections and build alliances with local communities. This soft approach allowed for a gradual integration of Islamic beliefs and practices into the fabric of Sudanese society. As Islam began to take root in the Sudan region, it started to attract followers among the local population. Converts to the new faith played a crucial role in furthering the influence of Islam and paving the way for more concerted efforts to expand the religion's reach. Over time, mosques and Islamic schools were established, providing centers for religious education and communal gatherings. The initial Islamic incursions into Sudan set the stage for the more structured and organized military campaigns. These early interactions laid the groundwork for future conquests by building alliances, spreading the message of Islam, and creating a network of support among the local population. The gradual nature of these incursions allowed for a more seamless transition to full-scale military campaigns, ensuring greater chances of success in the long run.

KEY BATTLES AND CAMPAIGNS IN THE SUDAN CONQUEST

The early Islamic incursions into the Sudan region were met with fierce resistance from indigenous tribes and kingdoms. One of the key battles during the Sudan conquest was the Battle of Dongola in 652 AD, where the Rashidun Caliphate forces, led by Abdullah ibn Saad, emerged victorious against the Nubian forces. This pivotal battle marked the beginning of Islamic dominance in the region. Another significant campaign was the Siege of Soba in 652 AD, where the Rashidun forces, under the command of Abdallah ibn Sa'd, besieged and captured the city of Soba, a major center of the Nubian kingdom of Alodia. The fall of Soba solidified Islamic control in the region and paved the way for further expansion. The Battle of Haldon in 652 AD was another crucial engagement during the Sudan conquest. The Rashidun forces, led by Abdullah ibn Saad, decisively defeated the Nubian armies, securing their hold over the region and opening up new territories for conquest. The Campaign of Kordofan in 653 AD was a strategic move by the Rashidun Caliphate to extend its influence into the western Sudan region. Led by Abdallah ibn Sa'd, the campaign resulted in the submission of the local tribes and establishing Islamic rule in Kordofan. Military campaigns, diplomatic negotiations, and alliances with local tribes and kingdoms marked the conquest of Sudan. The integration of various ethnic groups and cultural practices into the Islamic administration helped stabilize the region and ensure the long-term success of the conquest.

SOCIO-POLITICAL CHANGES IN SUDAN POST-CONQUEST

Islamic forces' conquest of the Sudan brought about significant socio-political changes in the region. The establishment of Islamic rule altered the existing power structures and governance systems, paving the way for a new era in Sudanese history. One of the key changes was the introduction of Islamic legal and administrative frameworks, which replaced traditional governance systems. The Islamic conquest led to the spread of the Arabic language and culture in Sudan, influencing various aspects of society. This cultural exchange blended local traditions with Islamic practices, creating a unique regional identity. The adoption of Islam as the dominant religion also had a profound impact on social norms and customs, shaping the moral and ethical values of the Sudanese people. The Islamic conquest brought about a shift in political authority, with local rulers and tribal leaders either assimilating into the new administration or resisting the changes. The establishment of Islamic governance structures led to the centralization of power and the creation of a more organized system of governance. This transition increased stability and security in the region and improved infrastructure and public services. The integration of Sudan into the larger Islamic world also facilitated trade and cultural exchanges, further contributing to the region's development. Sudan became a hub for intellectual and artistic endeavors, attracting scholars, poets, and artists from across the Islamic world. This cultural renaissance enriched Sudanese society and introduced new ideas and perspectives to the region. Overall, the socio-political changes brought about by the Islamic conquest of Sudan laid the foundation for a new era of development and cultural exchange in the region. The fusion of Islamic and indigenous traditions created a diverse and vibrant society, shaping the identity of Sudan for centuries to come.

RELIGIOUS AND CULTURAL IMPACT OF ISLAM IN SUDAN

The spread of Islam in Sudan had a profound impact on the religious and cultural landscape of the region. As Islamic beliefs and practices permeated Sudanese society, they influenced daily life and traditions. One of the primary effects of the introduction of Islam was the establishment of a new religious framework that shaped the spiritual beliefs of the Sudanese people. Islam brought a set of rituals, customs, and beliefs that integrated into Sudanese culture. Prayer, fasting, almsgiving, and pilgrimage to Mecca became central tenets of the Islamic faith practiced by many Sudanese. The construction of mosques and other religious structures provided physical spaces for worship and community gatherings, further solidifying the presence of Islam in the region.

Furthermore, Islamic teachings influenced social norms and values in Sudan. Concepts such as justice, equality, and compassion were emphasized in Islamic teachings and began to shape the moral fabric of Sudanese society. Islamic principles also impacted legal systems and governance, with Islamic law, or Sharia, playing a role in administrating justice and social order in the conquered territories. The advent of Islam also led to the spread of Arabic language and script in Sudan. Arabic became the language of administration, commerce, and education, further cementing the cultural influence of Islam in the region. Literature, poetry, and historical texts written in Arabic flourished in Sudan, contributing to preserving and disseminating knowledge and culture.

Moreover, blending indigenous traditions and Islamic practices gave rise to a unique Sudanese culture that combined elements of both worlds. Islamic festivals, such as Eid al-Fitr and Eid al-Adha, became celebrated alongside traditional Sudanese festivals, creating a rich tapestry of cultural heritage in the region. This cultural fusion diversified Sudanese society and fostered a sense of unity and shared identity among its diverse population. Overall, Islam's religious and cultural impact in Sudan profoundly shaped the region's beliefs, practices, and societal norms for centuries to come. Integrating Islamic teachings into Sudanese culture transformed the spiritual landscape and contributed to developing a rich and diverse cultural heritage that continues to define Sudanese identity today.

ADMINISTRATION AND GOVERNANCE IN THE CONQUERED TERRITORIES

The administration and governance in the conquered territories following the Islamic conquest of the Sudan were meticulously structured to maintain order and facilitate the integration of the new regions into the expanding Islamic empire. Islamic principles and governance systems were implemented, focusing on administering justice, providing security, and overseeing the collection and distribution of resources. Governors and administrators were appointed to oversee various regions, ensuring that Islamic law was upheld and the needs of the local populations were met. These officials were often chosen for their knowledge of Islamic jurisprudence and their diplomatic skills, enabling them to navigate the diverse cultural and ethnic landscapes of the conquered territories. The administration of the conquered territories also involved the establishment of administrative centers and the construction of mosques, schools, and other infrastructure to support the needs of the local populations. This infrastructure symbolized Islamic authority and helped foster a sense of community and belonging among the newly conquered peoples. Taxes and tributes were collected from the conquered territories to sustain the empire and support its military campaigns. These revenues were carefully managed and distributed to ensure the population's well-being and the Islamic empire's continued expansion. In addition to governing the conquered territories, efforts were made to encourage the conversion of the local populations to Islam. Mosques and religious schools were established to teach the principles of Islam, and local customs and traditions were often incorporated into Islamic practice to facilitate the integration of the newly conquered territories into the larger Islamic community. Overall, the administration and governance of the conquered territories following the Islamic conquest of the Sudan were instrumental in shaping the region's social, cultural, and political landscape, laying the foundations for the enduring legacy of Islam in the Sudan region.

RESISTANCE AND REBELLIONS IN THE SUDAN REGION

The Sudan region saw various resistance and rebellions following the Islamic conquests. The indigenous populations, deeply rooted in their own traditions and systems of governance, often resisted the imposition of Islamic rule. One of the notable rebellions was the Revolt of the Berbers, led by the indigenous tribes who rejected the Arab-Islamic administration. These rebellions were isolated incidents and highlighted the region's broader struggle for autonomy and self-governance. The resistance movements were driven by a desire to preserve local cultures and traditions and by grievances against the oppressive practices of the conquerors. The resistance movements often comprised guerrilla warfare, ambushes, and raids on the Islamic armies. The rebels used their terrain knowledge and warfare skills to challenge the Islamic rulers' authority. Despite facing superior military forces, the rebellions persisted, highlighting the resilience and determination of the local populations. The Islamic conquerors faced significant challenges in quelling these rebellions and maintaining control over the Sudan region. The successive waves of resistance forced the conquerors to adopt new strategies and tactics to suppress the rebellious populations. The ongoing conflicts not only strained the resources of the Islamic armies but also sowed seeds of discontent and instability in the conquered territories. The resistance movements in the Sudan region left a lasting impact on the Islamic conquests, shaping the dynamics of power and authority in the region. These rebellions became symbols of defiance against foreign domination and inspired future generations to resist external forces seeking to impose their will on the indigenous populations. The legacy of the resistance movements continues to resonate in the collective memory of the Sudan region, reminding people of the enduring spirit of resistance and resilience in the face of adversity.

LEGACY OF THE SUDAN CONQUEST

The legacy of the Sudan Conquest continues to shape the region's history and identity. The integration of Islam into Sudanese society following the conquest brought about significant changes in various aspects of life, including religion, culture, governance, and more. The population's embrace of Islam established Islamic law and customs that influenced legal systems, social norms, and daily practices. The Sudan Conquest also had a lasting impact on the region's political landscape. Establishing Islamic governance structures and integrating Sudan into the wider Islamic world facilitated trade, diplomacy, and cultural exchange. The caliphate's rule over Sudan fostered connections with other Islamic empires and strengthened ties within the Muslim community.

Furthermore, the legacy of the Sudan Conquest is evident in the region's architecture, art, and literature. The introduction of Islamic artistic styles, such as calligraphy, geometric patterns, and arabesques, influenced Sudanese art and architecture. Islamic education and scholarship flourished, leading to advancements in various fields, including science, medicine, and philosophy. Despite the profound impact of the Sudan Conquest, it also gave rise to resistance and rebellions among segments of the population who opposed the new order. These movements sought to preserve indigenous traditions, resist foreign influence, or challenge the legitimacy of the ruling authorities. While these rebellions were often met with force and suppression, they also highlighted the complexities and tensions inherent in the process of conquest and assimilation. In conclusion, the legacy of the Sudan Conquest is multifaceted and enduring. It has left a lasting imprint on the region's history, culture, and identity, shaping the trajectory of Sudanese society for centuries to come. The interplay of conquest, resistance, and adaptation reflects the dynamic and evolving nature of historical processes, illustrating the complexities of power, culture, and identity in the context of empire-building.

REFERENCES

Arabic

. مكي شبيكة. (1991). السودان عبر القرون. دار الجيل
. عبد المجيد عابدين. (1967). تاريخ الثقافة العربية في السودان. دار الثقافة
يوسف فضل حسن. (1967). مقدمة في تاريخ الممالك الإسلامية في السودان الشرقي. دار الجيل.
يوسف فضل حسن. (1989). دراسات في تاريخ السودان. جامعة الخرطوم.
الطيب محمد الطيب. (2000). الإسلام والقبائل العربية في السودان. مركز عبد الكريم ميرغني الثقافي.
. الشاطر بصيلي عبد الجليل. (1969). تاريخ وحضارة السودان. دار المعارف
. محمد إبراهيم أبو سليم. (1979). الحركة الفكرية في المهدية. دار الجيل
عبد الله علي إبراهيم. (2008). الصوفية والسياسة في السودان. مركز دراسات الوحدة العربية .

French

Cuoq, J. (1975). Les musulmans en Afrique. Maisonneuve et Larose.
Cuoq, J. M. (1986). Islamisation de la Nubie chrétienne (VIIe-XVIe siècle). Geuthner.
Godlewski, W. (1995). The Birth of Nubian Art: Some Remarks. In Actes de la VIIIe Conférence Internationale des Études Nubiennes (pp. 253-256). Lille.
Grandin, N. (1997). Le Soudan nilotique et l'administration britannique (1898-1956). Brill.
Millet, N. (1964). Les Nubiens et la Christianisation de la Nubie. Bulletin de l'Institut Français d'Archéologie Orientale, 64, 95-106.
Rilly, C. (2010). Le méroïtique et sa famille linguistique. Peeters.

Triaud, J. L., & Robinson, D. (2000). La Tijâniyya: Une confrérie musulmane à la conquête de l'Afrique. Karthala.

Vantini, G. (1981). Le Christianisme dans la Nubie ancienne. Pontificio Istituto Orientale.

English

Adams, W. Y. (1977). Nubia: Corridor to Africa. Princeton University Press.

Hasan, Y. F. (1967). The Arabs and the Sudan: From the Seventh to the Early Sixteenth Century. Edinburgh University Press.

Holt, P. M., & Daly, M. W. (2011). A History of the Sudan: From the Coming of Islam to the Present Day (6th ed.). Routledge.

Insoll, T. (2003). The Archaeology of Islam in Sub-Saharan Africa. Cambridge University Press.

McHugh, N. (1994). Holy Men of the Blue Nile: The Making of an Arab-Islamic Community in the Nilotic Sudan, 1500-1850. Northwestern University Press.

O'Fahey, R. S., & Spaulding, J. L. (1974). Kingdoms of the Sudan. Methuen.

Spaulding, J., & Kapteijns, L. (1991). The Spread of Islam in the Sudan. In N. Levtzion & R. L. Pouwels (Eds.), The History of Islam in Africa (pp. 119-141). Ohio University Press.

Vantini, G. (1975). Oriental Sources Concerning Nubia. Polish Academy of Sciences.

Welsby, D. A. (2002). The Medieval Kingdoms of Nubia: Pagans, Christians and Muslims Along the Middle Nile. British Museum Press.

Further Research

(Ferhat, 2018)Dierk Lange, "Progrès de l'Islam et Changement Politique au Kānem du XIe au XIIIe Siècle: Un Essai d'Intérpretation", The Journal of African History, Vol. 19 (1978), pp. 495-513.

This paper discusses the progress of Islam and political changes in Kanem (part of modern Chad/Sudan) from the 11th to 13th centuries.

(Brouwers, 1994)I. Ba, "La problématique de la présence juive au Sahara et au Soudan d'après Jean Léon l'Africain", Lagos Historical Review, Vol. 5 (2005), pp. 146-176.

While focused on Jewish presence, this article also discusses Islamic trade networks in Sudan during the late Middle Ages.

(Lecomte, 1974)Djibo Hamáni, "L'islam au Soudan central : histoire de l'islam au Niger du VIIe au XIXe siècle" (2007)

This book covers the history of Islam in central Sudan from the 7th to 19th centuries.

(Hmidi, 1993)H. Raulix, "Un aspect historique des rapports de l'animisme et de l'Islam au Niger", Journal Des Africanistes, Vol. 32 (1962), pp. 249-274.

This article examines historical aspects of the relationship between animism and Islam in Niger, which may have relevance for Sudan as well.

(Madjid, 2020): محمد عمر محمود, "الإسلام و المسيحية في القرن الإفريقي (السودان و إثيوبيا و الصومال)" (2014)

This book discusses Islam and Christianity in the Horn of Africa, including Sudan.

These sources provide a good starting point for researching the spread of Islam into Sudan from different perspectives and time periods. The English and French sources offer detailed historical analyses, while the Arabic source provides a broader regional context.

Bibliography:

Antoine, P. (2009). Comportements matrimoniaux au Sénégal à l'interface des traditions, de l'islam, de la colonisation et de la loi (18ème-20ème siècle). 237–252.

Asri, F. E. (2012). Vocabulaire théologico-mystique de l'islam et particularismes du lexique confrérique des Hmadcha.

Ba, I. (2005). La problématique de la présence juive au Sahara et au Soudan dáprès Jean Léon lÁfricain. Lagos Historical Review, 5, 146–176.

Bader, C. (2013). Un isolat surmique au Soudan du Sud: les Tennet.

Baumont, J. (1976). Une Source de l'Histoire du XIX° et du Début du XX° Siècle: Archives et Publications de l'Oeuvre de la Propagation de la Foi. History in Africa, 3, 164–170.

Berque, J. (1981). Histoire sociale de l'Islam contemporain.

Hamáni, D. (2007). L'islam au Soudan central: histoire de l'islam au Niger du VIIe au XIXe siècle.

Heer, N. L., & Makdisi, G. (1971). Ibn 'Aqīl et la Résurgence de l'Islam Traditionaliste au XIe Siècle (Ve siècle de l'Hégire) . Journal of the American Oriental Society, 91, 331.

Hmidi, L. (1993). Les aspects sociaux et politiques de la diffusion de l'Islam au Mali et au Songhai, 14-16e siècles.

Lange, D. (1978). Progrès de l'Islam et Changement Politique au Kānem du XIe au XIIIe Siècle: Un Essai d'Intérpretation. The Journal of African History, 19, 495–513.

Lecomte, G. (1965). George MAKDISI, Ibn 'Aqīl et la résurgence de l'Islam traditionaliste au XIe siècle (Ve siècle de l'Hégire), XXXIV + 602 pp., PIFD, Damas 1963.

Lecomte, G. (1974). Barbara STEPNIEWSKA, Rozpowszechnianie sįç Islamu w Sudanie Zachodnim od XII do XVI wieku (= L'expansion de l'Islam au Soudan Occidental du XIIe au XVIe siècles), 120 pp., Wroclaw 1972. Arabica, 21, 104–104.

McDougall, J. (2018). Laïcité, sociologie et histoire contemporaine de l'islam. Annales: Histoire, Sciences Sociales, 73, 411–439.

Miran, M. (2013). L'islam au sud de la savane. Anthropologie des sociétés musulmanes en Afrique de l'Ouest atlantique.

Moussa, S. (2013). "Relever en Égypte la dignité de la Patrie et de l'Islam". Pierre Loti et Moustapha Kamel, autour de 'La Mort de Philæ.'

Ouedraogo, A. (1996). L'enseignement de l'arabe et de l'islam en pays Mossi (Haute-Volta / Burkina Faso).

Raulix, H. (1962). Un aspect historique des rapports de l'animisme et de l'Islam au Niger. Journal Des Africanistes, 32, 249–274.

religioni, A. (2010). Histoire de l'Islam.

Şaul, M., & Benguigui, M. (2006). Le fanga comme savoir et destinée: Signification sociale de la réussite personnelle au Soudan occidental.

Schiettecatte, J. (2012). L'Arabie à l'aube de l'islam.

Schiettecatte, J., & Robin, C. (2009). L'Arabie à la veille de l'Islam. Un bilan clinique.

Torabi, D. (1994). Le miroir de mahomet; l'islam des recits de voyage francais en orient dans la seconde moitie du dix-septieme siecle.

Vincent, B. (1986). Entre la Chrétienté et l'Islam: le royaume de Grenade au XVIe siècle.

محمود, م. ع. (2014). الإسلام و المسيحية في القرن الإفريقي: السودان و إثيوبيا و الصومال = Islam and Christianity in the Horn of Africa: Somalia, Ethiopia, Sudan / Haggai Erlich. 36, 152–156.

V

EASTWARD EXPANSION: THE HORN OF AFRICA

THE HORN OF AFRICA

Stretching across the eastern coast of Africa lies a region of rich diversity and historical significance - the Horn of Africa. Comprising countries such as Ethiopia, Somalia, Djibouti, Eritrea, and parts of Sudan and Kenya, this area has long been a crossroads of cultures, religions, and trade. Its strategic location at the entrance to the Red Sea and proximity to the Arabian Peninsula made it a crucial gateway for trade between Africa, the Middle East, and beyond. The Horn of Africa is a land of contrasts, with its rugged mountains, arid deserts, fertile highlands, and bustling coastal cities. Its diverse geography has shaped the unique cultures and societies that have thrived in this region for centuries. From the ancient civilizations of Axum and Kush to the vibrant trade networks that connected the region to the broader world, the Horn of Africa has played a pivotal role in shaping the history of the African continent. As Islamic expansion spread across North Africa and into the

Middle East, the Horn of Africa emerged as a key frontier for the new religion. The region's proximity to the Arabian Peninsula and established trade routes made it an attractive target for early Islamic conquests. The interactions between the indigenous peoples of the Horn and the expanding Islamic caliphates laid the groundwork for a complex and transformative chapter in the region's history. As we delve into the early Islamic encounters in the Horn of Africa, we will explore the power, trade, and religious exchange dynamics that shaped the region during this period of profound change. By examining the interconnected histories of the peoples of the Horn and the Islamic world, we can gain a deeper understanding of the forces that drove the expansion of Islam into this diverse and dynamic region.

EARLY ISLAMIC ENCOUNTERS IN THE HORN

Refuge in Abyssinia (Ethiopia):

During the early years of Islam, around 615 AD, a group of Muslims sought refuge from persecution in Mecca by fleeing to the Christian Kingdom of Abyssinia (modern-day Ethiopia), ruled by a king known as the Najashi or Negus. This significant event marks one of the first contacts between Islam and the Horn of Africa. The Najashi is famously known for protecting these early Muslims, respecting their faith, and refusing to extradite them to the Quraysh of Mecca.

Trade and Cultural Exchanges:

Following this initial contact, there were increased interactions between the Islamic world and the Horn of Africa, primarily through trade. The Red Sea and the Nile River served as important trade routes that facilitated the exchange of goods and cultural and religious ideas between the Arabian Peninsula and the Horn of Africa.

Military Campaigns and Political Alliances:

As early as the 7th century, Islamic forces began to establish a presence in the region through trade and peaceful interactions with local tribes.

During those years, particularly during the caliphates of Umayyad and Abbasid, several military campaigns were aimed at bringing the regions of the Horn under Islamic political influence. These efforts were met with varying success and resistance from local Christian kingdoms.

By the medieval period, several Islamic sultanates, such as the Sultanate of Adal, had been established in the Horn of Africa. These sultanates played crucial roles in spreading Islam in the region through peaceful conversion and military conquests. The interactions between these Islamic sultanates and the Christian Ethiopian empire were marked by both trade and conflict.

The coastal areas of modern-day Somalia and Djibouti were among the first to experience these early Islamic encounters. Arab traders and missionaries played a crucial role in spreading the teachings of Islam to the Horn of Africa. They established small communities along the coast and engaged in cultural exchanges with the local populations. These interactions laid the groundwork for the later expansion of Islamic influence in the region. One of the key figures in these early Islamic encounters was the legendary explorer and merchant Ibn Battuta. In the 14th century, Ibn Battuta traveled extensively throughout the Horn of Africa, documenting his experiences and interactions with the locals. His writings provide valuable insights into the region's social, political, and religious dynamics during this period. Islamic scholars and theologians also significantly contributed to Islam's spread in the Horn of Africa. They engaged in intellectual debates with local religious leaders and converted many to the Islamic faith through their teachings and writings. The establishment of mosques and madrasas further solidified the presence of Islam in the region. Despite resistance from some indigenous groups and traditional religious practices, Islam gradually gained a foothold in the Horn of Africa through trade, diplomacy, and cultural exchange. These early Islamic encounters set the stage for the strategic importance of the Horn in the larger context of Islamic expansion and conquests across Africa.

THE STRATEGIC IMPORTANCE OF THE HORN IN ISLAMIC EXPANSION

The strategic significance of the Horn of Africa in the Islamic expansion cannot be overstated. It served as a crucial gateway for the spread of Islam into the region and beyond, linking the Islamic heartlands with the diverse lands of East Africa. The Horn's location at the crossroads of trade routes connecting the Red Sea, Indian Ocean, and the Mediterranean made it a highly coveted region for Islamic rulers and merchants. The Horn of Africa's coastline provided access to key trade routes and facilitated the movement of goods, people, and ideas between the Islamic world and East Africa. The port cities along the coast, such as Mogadishu, Mombasa, and Aden, became vibrant centers of economic activity, cultural exchange, and Islamic learning.

Moreover, the Horn's proximity to the Arabian Peninsula made it a strategic outpost for Islamic powers seeking to expand their regional influence. Control over the Horn allowed Islamic rulers to project power into East Africa, exert control over trade networks, and establish alliances with local rulers. The Horn of Africa's diverse and complex political landscape presented opportunities and challenges for Islamic expansion. Local kingdoms and city-states in the region often resisted Islamic rule, leading to protracted conflicts and military campaigns. The rugged terrain, harsh climate, and formidable warriors of the area made it a problematic battleground for Islamic armies. Despite these challenges, Islamic rulers established control over key territories in the Horn of Africa through military conquest, diplomacy, and cultural exchange. The adoption of Islam by local elites and the gradual spread of Islamic practices and institutions helped to integrate the region into the wider Islamic world. In conclusion, the Horn of Africa played a pivotal role in the Islamic expansion, serving as a gateway for the spread of Islam into East Africa and beyond. Its strategic importance as a crossroads of trade, culture, and politics shaped the trajectory of Islamic expansion in the region and left a lasting legacy of Islamic influence in the Horn.

CHALLENGES FACED IN THE HORN

The Horn of Africa presented a unique set of challenges for the Islamic expansion. One of the primary obstacles faced in this region was the geographical landscape. With its rugged terrain and inhospitable climates, traversing the Horn proved daunting for the Muslim forces. The arid deserts and mountainous regions posed significant logistical challenges, making mobilizing troops and maintaining supply lines difficult. Moreover, the diverse and fragmented nature of the local populations in the Horn added another layer of complexity to the conquest efforts. Unlike the more centralized empires in other regions, the Horn was characterized by numerous tribal and ethnic groups with distinct cultures and alliances. This decentralized structure made it challenging for the Islamic forces to establish a united front and negotiate treaties with the various factions.

Furthermore, the Horn of Africa was also known for its fierce resistance to foreign invaders. The local tribes and kingdoms had a long history of defending their territories against external threats, using guerrilla warfare tactics and knowledge of the terrain to their advantage. This fierce sense of independence and resistance posed a significant challenge to the Islamic forces attempting to assert their regional dominance. The Horn of Africa's strategic location at the crossroads of trade routes and maritime navigation further complicated the conquest efforts. Control over key ports and trading hubs was essential for sustaining the Islamic empire's economic interests in the region. However, competing interests from other regional powers and pirates made establishing a secure foothold and maintaining control over vital trade routes challenging. Despite these challenges, the Islamic forces persevered in their campaigns in the Horn of Africa, adapting their strategies to overcome the obstacles they encountered. Through military prowess, diplomatic negotiations, and cultural integration, the Muslims could gradually extend their influence and establish a lasting presence in this strategically important region.

MILITARY CAMPAIGNS IN THE HORN

The military campaigns in the Horn of Africa presented a unique set of challenges for the Islamic forces. The rugged terrain and harsh climate made advancement difficult, requiring strategic planning and adaptability. The presence of local tribes and kingdoms added complexity to the campaigns, as rivalries and alliances had to be carefully navigated. Islamic armies faced resistance from formidable local leaders determined to protect their lands from foreign invaders. Battles were fought with courage and determination, with casualties mounting. The Islamic forces had to employ tactics, including siege warfare, guerilla tactics, and diplomatic negotiations, to gain a foothold in the region. Despite the challenges faced, the military campaigns in the Horn of Africa were marked by moments of triumph and conquest. Through perseverance and strategic maneuvering, the Islamic forces made significant territorial gains and established control over key strategic locations. These campaigns showcased the Islamic warriors' skill, determination, and ability to adapt to diverse and challenging environments. As the military campaigns unfolded, alliances were forged with local leaders who saw the benefits of cooperation with the Islamic forces. These alliances played a crucial role in the success of the campaigns, enabling the Islamic armies to overcome obstacles and secure essential victories. The Islamic forces expanded their influence in the Horn of Africa through military might and diplomatic finesse. They laid the groundwork for the region's integration into the Islamic empire. The military campaigns in the Horn of Africa left a lasting impact on the area, shaping its history and culture for centuries to come. The lessons learned from these campaigns, including the importance of strategic planning, adaptability, and diplomacy, continue to resonate in the annals of Islamic conquests.

DIPLOMATIC ENGAGEMENTS WITH LOCAL LEADERS

Within the Horn of Africa, diplomatic engagements were crucial in spreading and consolidating Islamic influence during the early medieval period. Muslim leaders, recognizing the region's diversity and the need for strategic alliances, actively pursued diplomatic relationships with local rulers and communities. These diplomatic engagements were multifaceted and tailored to the specific circumstances of each region. Muslim envoys often sought to establish trade agreements, secure safe passage for merchants and travelers, and forge alliances against common enemies. Muslim leaders established peaceful relations with local leaders through these diplomatic efforts, promoting regional stability and cooperation.

In many cases, these engagements involved negotiations regarding the status of non-Muslim communities under Islamic rule. Muslim leaders, recognizing the importance of religious diversity in the region, often granted autonomy to non-Muslim communities, allowing them to practice their faith and maintain their cultural identity. This approach helped to foster tolerance and coexistence among different religious and ethnic groups in the Horn of Africa. Furthermore, diplomatic engagements with local leaders also facilitated the spread of Islamic culture and ideas in the region. Local rulers often welcomed Muslim scholars and teachers who recognized the potential benefits of Islamic education and learning. Through these exchanges, Islamic principles of governance, law, and scholarship gradually permeated the societies of the Horn of Africa, shaping their political and cultural landscapes. Overall, diplomatic engagements with local leaders were instrumental in the integration of the Horn of Africa into the broader Islamic world. By fostering dialogue, cooperation, and understanding, Muslim leaders established lasting relationships with the region's diverse communities, laying the foundation for the enduring legacy of Islamic influence in the Horn of Africa.

RELIGIOUS AND CULTURAL IMPACTS OF ISLAMIC EXPANSION

The expansion of Islam into the Horn of Africa had profound religious and cultural impacts on the region. As Islamic forces moved into these territories, they brought their faith and a rich tapestry of traditions, practices, and beliefs. The introduction of Islam fundamentally transformed the Horn's religious landscape, shaping its inhabitants' spiritual outlook for generations to come. With its monotheistic beliefs and emphasis on social justice, Islam provided a new framework for understanding the world and one's place in it. The teachings of the Quran and the Hadiths served as a guiding light for the people of the Horn, offering moral guidance and ethical principles to govern their lives. The establishment of mosques and madrasas allowed for the spread of Islamic knowledge and the cultivation of a learned religious class within the region. In addition to its spiritual influence, the expansion of Islam also had a profound cultural impact on the Horn of Africa. The Arabic language, as the language of the Quran, became a vehicle for disseminating Islamic teachings and a unifying force among diverse ethnolinguistic groups. Arabic script was introduced and used for religious and administrative purposes, fostering a literary tradition that continues today.

Moreover, the Islamic expansion facilitated the exchange of ideas, technologies, and cultural practices between the Horn and the wider Islamic world. The architecture of mosques and other Islamic monuments reflected a fusion of local building styles with Islamic motifs, creating a distinct regional architectural heritage. Trade networks established through Islamic connections brought new goods, commodities, and artistic influences to the Horn, enriching its material culture and stimulating economic development. Ultimately, Islamic expansion's religious and cultural impacts in the Horn of Africa were far-reaching and transformative. They laid the foundation for a dynamic and diverse Islamic civilization that continues to shape the region's identity today.

INTEGRATION OF THE HORN INTO THE ISLAMIC EMPIRE

Integrating the Horn of Africa into the Islamic Empire was a gradual and complex process that blended cultures, traditions, and governance systems. As Islamic influence spread throughout the region, local societies underwent significant transformations, adopting new religious practices, legal systems, and architectural styles. One of the key mechanisms of integration was the establishment of Islamic administrative structures in major urban centers such as Mogadishu, Zeila, and Harar. These cities became hubs of Islamic learning, trade, and governance, attracting scholars, merchants, and administrators from across the Islamic world. Islamic legal principles, known as Sharia, were also introduced and implemented in the Horn of Africa, influencing the local legal systems and social norms. This integration of Sharia law facilitated the resolution of disputes, the administration of justice, and the regulation of societal conduct by Islamic principles.

Furthermore, the construction of mosques, madrassas, and other Islamic architectural landmarks symbolized the permanence of Islamic influence in the region. These structures served as places of worship and as centers of education, community gathering, and artistic expression. The integration of the Horn of Africa into the Islamic Empire was not without its challenges, as local resistance, cultural differences, and political rivalries sometimes hindered the process. However, the Islamic Empire established a lasting presence in the region through military conquests, diplomatic engagements, and cultural exchanges. As a result of this integration, the Horn of Africa experienced a profound transformation, with Islam becoming a dominant cultural and religious force. The legacy of Islamic influence in the region can be seen in various aspects of society, from language and architecture to food, music, and art. The integration of the Horn of Africa into the Islamic Empire reshaped the region's identity. It connected it to the broader Islamic world, contributing to the diversity and richness of Islamic civilization.

LEGACY OF ISLAMIC INFLUENCE IN THE HORN

The legacy of Islamic influence in the Horn of Africa is profound and enduring. From the moment Muslim armies set foot in the region, they brought with them a rich tapestry of culture, language, and religion that would forever shape the identity of the Horn. The integration of the Horn into the Islamic Empire during the early medieval period marked the beginning of a transformation that would leave an indelible mark on the region. The most visible legacy of Islamic influence in the Horn can be seen in its architecture and urban planning. The introduction of Islamic architectural styles, such as mosques adorned with intricate geometric patterns and calligraphy, transformed the region's landscape. Cities like Harar in present-day Ethiopia became centers of Islamic learning and culture, attracting scholars and traders worldwide. In addition to architecture, the spread of Islam in the Horn profoundly impacted the region's language and literature. Arabic, as the language of the Quran, became a prestigious language of religious and scholarly study, leading to the development of a rich literary tradition in the region. This linguistic exchange enriched the cultural tapestry of the Horn and facilitated trade and communication with the wider Islamic world. The legacy of Islamic influence in the Horn is also evident in the region's social and political structures. Establishing Islamic legal and administrative systems provided a framework for governance that incorporated local customs and traditions. Islamic principles of justice, charity, and equality influenced the development of legal codes and social norms in the region, shaping the moral fabric of Horn societies.

Furthermore, the spread of Islam in the Horn brought with it a new set of values and beliefs that continue to shape the region today. The emphasis on unity, brotherhood, and submission to the will of Allah fostered a sense of community and shared identity among the diverse peoples of the Horn. This sense of unity transcended ethnic and tribal boundaries, creating a common bond that endures despite the passage of centuries. In conclusion, the legacy of Islamic influence in the Horn of Africa is a testament to the enduring power of cultural exchange and adaptation. Through architecture, language, literature, governance, and values, Islam has left an indelible mark on the region, shaping its identity and enriching its cultural heritage. The integration of the Horn into the Islamic Empire was not just a conquest but a transformation that continues to resonate in the vibrant tapestry of the Horn's history and culture.

CONCLUSION: THE HORN OF AFRICA IN THE CONTEXT OF ISLAMIC CONQUESTS

The Islamic conquests in the Horn of Africa have left a lasting impact on the region, profoundly shaping its history, culture, and society. The legacy of Islamic influence in the Horn is evident in various aspects of life, from architecture and language to religion and trade. The spread of Islam in the region brought new ideas, technologies, and practices that transformed the social fabric of the Horn and connected it to the broader Islamic world. The Islamic conquests also paved the way for the establishment of powerful empires and states in the region, such as the Sultanate of Adal and the Adal Kingdom, which played a significant role in shaping the political landscape of the Horn. Islamic conquests in the Horn of Africa not only resulted in the spread of Islam but also facilitated the exchange of goods, ideas, and knowledge between the Horn and other parts of the Islamic world. This cultural exchange enriched the region and contributed to its growth and development in various fields, including architecture, literature, and art. The influence of Islamic civilization can still be seen in the diverse architectural styles, the Arabic script used in writing, and the customs and traditions practiced in the Horn today. Overall, the Islamic conquests in the Horn of Africa have left a lasting legacy that continues to shape the region today. The integration of Islamic culture and traditions into the fabric of Horn societies has created a unique blend of influences that define the region's identity. By understanding the historical context of the Islamic conquests in the Horn of Africa, we can appreciate the rich cultural tapestry woven through centuries of interaction and exchange between the peoples of the Horn and the broader Islamic world.

The integration of the Horn of Africa into the Islamic world was not just political but also involved significant cultural and religious syncretism. The region saw the emergence of a unique blend of Islamic and local African traditions.

The Horn of Africa became an integral part of the Islamic trade network, connecting it with the Middle East, North

Africa, and Asia. Cities like Zeila became bustling trade centers where goods and cultures mingled.

The region contributed scholars and religious figures to the broader Islamic intellectual world. This included the transmission of Islamic knowledge and the establishment of religious schools.

REFERENCES

Arabic:

الحسن بن أحمد الهمداني (1884). صفة جزيرة العرب. Brill.

ابن حوقل (1938). صورة الأرض. Dar Sader Publishers.

المسعودي (1965). مروج الذهب ومعادن الجوهر. Dar Al-Andalus.

الإدريسي (1989). نزهة المشتاق في اختراق الآفاق. Alam Al-Kutub.

ياقوت الحموي (1977). معجم البلدان. Dar Sader Publishers.

أحمد بن فضل الله العمري (2010). مسالك الأبصار في ممالك الأمصار. Al-Majma' Al-Thaqafi.

القلقشندي (1914). صبح الأعشى في صناعة الإنشا. Dar Al-Kutub Al-Misriyya.

English:

Behera, M. N. (2011). Interfaith Relations after One Hundred Years: Christian Mission among Other Faiths.

Cuoq, Joseph (1981). "L'Islam en Éthiopie: des origines au XVIe siècle." Nouvelles Éditions Latines.

Erlich, Haggai (1994). "Ethiopia and the Middle East." Lynne Rienner Publishers.

Gilbert, E., & Reynolds, J. T. (2003). Africa in World History: From Prehistory to the Present.

Insoll, Timothy (2003). "The Archaeology of Islam in Sub-Saharan Africa." Cambridge University Press.

Kapteijns, Lidwien (2000). "Ethiopia and the Horn of Africa." In "The History of Islam in Africa," edited by Nehemia Levtzion and Randall L. Pouwels. Ohio University Press.

Lewis, I.M. (1988). "A Modern History of Somalia: Nation and State in the Horn of Africa." Westview Press.

Loimeier, Roman (2013). "Muslim Societies in Africa: A Historical Anthropology." Indiana University Press.

Robinson, David (2004). "Muslim Societies in African History." Cambridge University Press.

Rue, G. M. L. (n.d.). Slave Trades and Diaspora in the Middle East, 700 to 1900 CE. In Oxford Research Encyclopedia of African History.

Seligman, A. (2012). A Review of "Islam and Christianity in the Horn of Africa: Somalia, Ethiopia, Sudan." History: Reviews of New Books, 40, 121–121.

Singleton, B. D. (2009). "That Ye May Know Each Other": Late Victorian Interactions between British and West African Muslims. Journal of Muslim Minority Affairs, 29, 369–385.

Trimingham, J.S. (1952). "Islam in Ethiopia." Oxford University Press.

VI

CONSOLIDATION AND ADMINISTRATION

ESTABLISHING GOVERNANCE STRUCTURES

Establishing governance structures during the Islamic conquests in Africa was crucial in ensuring effective administration and control over the newly acquired territories. These structures were designed to uphold the principles of Islamic law and facilitate the smooth functioning of the state. At the heart of the governance system was the appointment of an Amir or ruler who served as the supreme authority in the region. The Amir was responsible for overseeing all aspects of governance, including justice, security, and public welfare. They were often appointed by the Caliph or a higher-ranking official and were expected to govern by Islamic principles. Under the leadership of the Amir, various administrative positions were established to manage different aspects of governance. These positions included judges (Qadis) responsible for interpreting and enforcing Sharia law, tax collectors who ensured revenue collection for the state, and military commanders who maintained security and defended against external threats. Provincial administrations were also set up to facilitate governance at the local level. Each province was overseen by a Wali or governor who acted as the Amir's representative and was tasked with implementing policies and directives from the central government. The Wali worked closely with a council of advisors and officials to address local issues and ensure the efficient delivery of services to the population. In addition to formal governance structures, the Islamic rulers implemented systems of accountability and oversight to prevent corruption and abuse of power. Auditors were appointed to monitor the financial affairs of government officials, while watchdog committees were established to investigate complaints and ensure that justice was served fairly. Overall, establishing governance structures was essential in laying the foundation for effective administration during the Islamic conquests in Africa. Through these structures, the rulers could maintain order, uphold the principles of Sharia law, and govern the diverse populations of the newly conquered territories with efficiency and fairness.

IMPLEMENTATION OF SHARIA LAW

Islamic law, known as Sharia, played a pivotal role in shaping the governance structures of the newly conquered territories. Designed to provide a comprehensive framework for personal conduct and societal norms, Sharia governed various aspects of life, including social, economic, and legal matters. The implementation of Sharia law in these territories aimed to establish a sense of moral order and justice in line with Islamic principles. Under Sharia law, judges, known as qadis, were appointed to adjudicate legal disputes based on Islamic jurisprudence. These judges were tasked with interpreting and applying Sharia principles to resolve conflicts and ensure fair treatment for all individuals. Their decisions were binding and carried the weight of religious authority, helping to maintain law and order in the newly established administrations. In addition to the judicial system, Sharia law regulated personal conduct and public behavior, outlining marriage, inheritance, and commercial transactions guidelines. These regulations helped to foster a sense of community cohesion and adherence to Islamic values among the diverse population of the conquered territories.

Moreover, implementing Sharia law also served as a unifying factor, providing a common legal framework that transcended ethnic and cultural differences. By emphasizing the principles of justice, equality, and accountability, Sharia law helped to create a sense of shared identity and purpose among the residents of the newly administered provinces. Overall, the implementation of Sharia law played a crucial role in establishing a governance system rooted in Islamic principles and responsive to the practical needs of the conquered territories. Through its emphasis on justice, morality, and social cohesion, Sharia law contributed to the consolidation of political authority and the maintenance of order in the diverse and expansive territories of the Islamic empire.

FORMATION OF PROVINCIAL ADMINISTRATIONS

Establishing provincial administrations was a critical aspect of the Islamic conquests in Africa. The conquered territories were divided into smaller administrative units, each governed by a provincial administrator appointed by the central authority. These administrators, known as walis or governors, were responsible for the day-to-day governance of their respective provinces, ensuring the implementation of Islamic law, maintaining law and order, and overseeing the collection of taxes. The provincial administrations were tasked with upholding the caliphate's authority, fostering stability, and promoting economic development in their regions. They oversaw the distribution of resources, the management of public services such as education and healthcare, and the administration of justice. They also played a key role in managing relations with local non-Muslim populations, ensuring their rights and protection under Islamic law. One of the critical challenges faced by provincial administrators was balancing centralized control with local autonomy. While they were expected to enforce the dictates of the central authority, they also had to consider the unique cultural, social, and economic dynamics of their provinces. This necessitated a degree of flexibility and pragmatism in governance, allowing for adaptations to local conditions while maintaining fidelity to Islamic principles. Overall, the formation of provincial administrations played a crucial role in consolidating the Islamic conquests in Africa. By establishing effective governance structures at the local level, the caliphate could extend its influence, maintain order, and promote the spread of Islam throughout the conquered territories.

ECONOMIC POLICIES AND TRADE NETWORKS

Islamic authorities recognized the critical role of economic policies and trade networks in sustaining the newly conquered territories. A key aspect of their strategy was promoting trade and commerce, which facilitated economic growth and strengthened ties with other regions. Establishing stable trade routes and markets helped reduce the flow of goods and wealth throughout the empire. This boosted economic prosperity and fostered cultural exchange and cooperation among diverse communities. To regulate trade and ensure fairness, the Islamic administrators implemented policies to standardize weights and measures, enforce property rights, and maintain market integrity. This created a conducive environment for merchants and traders, encouraging economic activity and growth.

Developing a standard currency system also facilitated transactions and further promoted trade across the empire. Islamic rulers also invested in infrastructure projects to enhance trade networks, such as constructing roads, bridges, and ports. These initiatives facilitated the movement of goods, provided employment opportunities, and spurred economic development in various regions. Moreover, developing sophisticated irrigation systems and agricultural technologies boosted agricultural productivity, ensuring food security and financial stability. Trade networks were not only limited to local markets but extended to international trade routes, connecting the Islamic territories to distant lands. This facilitated the exchange of goods, ideas, and technologies, contributing to the prosperity and growth of the empire. The strategic location of key trade hubs, such as Cairo, Alexandria, and Tunis, played a crucial role in connecting the Islamic world to Europe, Asia, and Africa. Overall, the Islamic authorities' emphasis on economic policies and trade networks was instrumental in fostering economic prosperity, cultural exchange, and stability within the empire. Promoting trade, investing in infrastructure, and facilitating international commerce laid the foundation for a thriving economy that supported the diverse populations living under Islamic rule.

MANAGEMENT OF CULTURAL AND RELIGIOUS DIVERSITY

Managing cultural and religious diversity within the territories conquered during the Islamic expansion played a crucial role in maintaining stability and fostering coexistence among various communities. The Arab conquerors implemented a tolerance policy towards different religions and cultures, recognizing the traditions and practices of the indigenous populations—this inclusive approach aimed to facilitate peaceful integration and prevent social unrest. One of the key strategies employed was the recognition of religious freedom, allowing non-Muslims to practice their faith without fear of persecution. This policy not only respected the diverse beliefs of the conquered peoples but also fostered a sense of harmony and mutual respect within the newly established societies. Additionally, Islamic rulers often appointed local leaders to govern their communities, acknowledging the importance of indigenous customs and traditions in maintaining social cohesion. Art and architecture also played a significant role in promoting cultural diversity and unity within the Islamic territories. Blending local artistic styles with Islamic influences resulted in a vibrant cultural tapestry that reflected the multicultural nature of the society. This fusion of artistic traditions not only created a sense of collective identity but also served as a testament to the inclusive ethos of the Islamic rulers.

Furthermore, establishing educational institutions and centers of learning promoted intellectual exchange and dialogue among scholars from different backgrounds. These centers became hubs of cultural exchange, where ideas and knowledge were shared across religious and ethnic divides, contributing to the flourishing of arts, sciences, and philosophy. This intellectual exchange helped bridge cultural differences and fostered a spirit of cooperation and understanding among diverse communities. In conclusion, cultural and religious diversity management during the Islamic conquests was characterized by a policy of tolerance, respect, and inclusivity. By recognizing the diversity of beliefs and traditions within their territories, Islamic rulers created a harmonious and integrated society that celebrated the richness of its cultural heritage. This approach facilitated the peaceful coexistence of different communities and laid the foundation for a flourishing civilization that embraced the values of diversity and unity.

MILITARY GARRISONS AND SECURITY MEASURES

Military Garrisons and Security Measures: Military garrisons were strategically positioned throughout the newly conquered territories to maintain control and security. These garrisons served as strongholds from which the ruling authorities could quickly respond to any signs of unrest or rebellion. The presence of well-equipped troops instilled a sense of order and deterred potential challengers to the established power structure. Security measures were implemented to safeguard both the military garrisons and the local population. Patrols along crucial trade routes and borders helped prevent possible incursions by rival factions or nomadic groups. Fortifications were constructed to fortify vulnerable points and protect against external threats. Surveillance networks were established to gather intelligence and monitor suspicious activities. The selection and training of soldiers for the garrisons were rigorous processes designed to ensure the highest level of readiness and discipline. Commanders were chosen based on merit and proven leadership skills, focusing on maintaining unit morale and cohesion. Regular drills and exercises honed the troops' combat abilities and prepared them for any potential conflict. Collaboration with local communities was essential in maintaining the stability of the garrisons. Efforts were made to establish positive relationships with tribal leaders and influential figures to gain support and cooperation. Integrating elements of the local population into the garrisons fostered a sense of unity and shared purpose, strengthening the overall security apparatus. In times of crisis or external threat, the military garrisons played a crucial role in safeguarding the stability and integrity of the Islamic territories. Their presence was a visible symbol of authority and strength, deterring would-be aggressors and preserving the peace established through the conquests. Through strategic positioning, rigorous training, and effective collaboration, the military garrisons upheld the realm's security and ensured the Islamic administration's continued success.

INFRASTRUCTURE DEVELOPMENT AND URBAN PLANNING

In the wake of establishing military garrisons and ensuring security measures, the Islamic conquerors focused on infrastructure development and urban planning. They aimed to create well-organized and sustainable cities that could serve as governance, commerce, and culture centers. The conquered territories were transformed by constructing roads, bridges, and aqueducts, facilitating trade and communication between regions. Urban centers were carefully planned, with mosques, markets, and administrative buildings strategically located to promote efficiency and social cohesion. The conquerors also implemented advanced irrigation systems and agricultural techniques to maximize productivity and support the growing population. These efforts enhanced the residents' quality of life and solidified the conquerors' control over the newly acquired territories. The legacy of their infrastructure development and urban planning can still be seen in many parts of Africa today, a testament to the foresight and ingenuity of the Islamic conquerors.

COMMUNICATION AND TRANSPORTATION NETWORKS

The development of communication and transportation networks was crucial to ensuring efficient governance in the newly conquered territories. Roads and trade routes were expanded and improved to facilitate the movement of goods, people, and information across the vast expanse of the empire. Messenger services were established to enable swift communication between distant regions, allowing for the rapid transmission of orders and decrees from the central government to the provincial administrations. Additionally, constructing canals and bridges facilitated trade and commerce, further integrating the various regions under Islamic rule. These infrastructure developments enhanced the empire's connectivity and fostered economic growth and cultural exchange. By investing in communication and transportation networks, the Islamic Caliphate maintained its hegemony over a vast and diverse territory, ensuring the efficient administration of its holdings while promoting unity and cohesion among its subjects.

DIPLOMATIC RELATIONS WITH NON-MUSLIM COMMUNITIES

The establishment of diplomatic relations with non-Muslim communities was a crucial aspect of maintaining peace and stability within the expanding Islamic empire. The early Muslim leaders sought to ensure cooperation and peaceful coexistence with diverse populations through treaties, alliances, and negotiations. These diplomatic efforts were guided by justice, tolerance, and mutual respect. One of the key strategies employed by the Muslim rulers was granting autonomy to non-Muslim communities, allowing them to govern themselves according to their laws and customs. This approach not only preserved these communities' cultural and religious identity but also fostered a sense of loyalty and allegiance to the Islamic state. Diplomatic envoys were dispatched to neighboring regions to forge alliances and establish trade relations. These envoys, known as emissaries, negotiated treaties, resolved disputes, and promoted peaceful exchanges between different communities. By engaging in diplomatic dialogue and building diplomatic networks, the early Muslim leaders created a climate of trust and cooperation among diverse ethnic and religious groups.

Furthermore, the Islamic rulers encouraged interfaith dialogue and cultural exchange, recognizing the value of diversity in promoting social harmony and mutual understanding. Scholars, merchants, and artisans from different backgrounds were welcomed into the Islamic empire, contributing to a rich tapestry of ideas, traditions, and innovations. Overall, diplomatic relations with non-Muslim communities played a crucial role in maintaining the long-term stability of the Islamic empire, fostering peaceful coexistence, and promoting cooperation across cultural and religious boundaries. Through dialogue, negotiation, and respect for diversity, the early Muslim leaders set a precedent for diplomacy to shape history in the centuries to come.

EFFORTS TO ENSURE LONG-TERM STABILITY

Efforts to Ensure Long-Term Stability: Islamic rulers in Africa understood the importance of establishing stability to ensure the longevity of their rule and the prosperity of their territories. This stability was not only vital for the well-being of their Muslim subjects but also for the harmonious coexistence with non-Muslim communities. To achieve this long-term stability, several key efforts were made. One crucial aspect was maintaining strong diplomatic relations with neighboring kingdoms and empires. Islamic rulers sought to create a network of mutual support and cooperation by cultivating alliances and treaties with non-Muslim powers. This not only helped in averting potential conflicts but also fostered trade relations and cultural exchanges, contributing to the region's overall prosperity.

Furthermore, efforts were made to promote social cohesion and unity among the diverse populace of the Islamic realms. Policies were implemented to respect and protect the rights of non-Muslim communities, allowing them to practice their faith and customs freely. This inclusivity helped foster a sense of belonging and loyalty among all inhabitants, regardless of their religious beliefs. Another critical measure for long-term stability was the establishment of efficient administrative and legal systems. Islamic rulers invested in developing robust governance structures and implementing Sharia law to ensure justice and order in their territories. By providing a fair and consistent legal framework, they aimed to create a stable and predictable environment conducive to economic growth and social harmony.

Furthermore, infrastructure development and urban planning initiatives were undertaken to improve the quality of life for the population. Investments in public works, such as water management systems, roads, and marketplaces, enhanced the region's prosperity and facilitated communication and trade, strengthening the ties between different communities. Overall, the efforts to ensure long-term stability in Islamic Africa were multifaceted and comprehensive. Islamic rulers laid the foundation for the enduring prosperity and peace of their realms by prioritizing diplomatic relations, social inclusivity, effective governance, and infrastructure development.

REFERENCES

Arabic Sources:

Al-Baladhuri's "Kitab Futuh Al-Buldan" (Book of the Conquest of Lands) is a key classical Arabic source on the early Islamic conquests and administration. (Cebeci, 2022)

Al-Tabari's "Tarikh al-Rusul wa al-Muluk" (History of the Prophets and Kings) provides extensive accounts of administrative practices during the Islamic conquests. (Cebeci, 2022)

"الحكم الإسلامي في شمال أفريقيا" (Islamic Rule in North Africa) by a modern Arab historian examines the establishment of Islamic governance in North Africa. (Cebeci, 2022)

الزبيدي، محمد مرتضى. (1965). "تاج العروس من جواهر القاموس." الكويت: مطبعة حكومة الكويت.

ابن خلدون، عبد الرحمن. (2004). "المقدمة." بيروت: دار الفكر.

المقريزي، أحمد بن علي. (1998). "المواعظ والاعتبار بذكر الخطط والآثار." بيروت: دار الكتب العلمية.

السعدي، عبد الرحمن بن عبد الله. (1981). "تاريخ السودان." باريس: مكتبة أدريان ميزونوف.

الطبري، محمد بن جرير. (1967). "تاريخ الرسل والملوك." القاهرة: دار المعارف.

البكري، أبو عبيد. (1992). "المسالك والممالك." بيروت: دار الغرب الإسلامي.

الإدريسي، محمد بن محمد. (2002). "نزهة المشتاق في اختراق الآفاق." القاهرة: مكتبة الثقافة الدينية.

English Sources:

ʿAzīz Dūrī, ʿAbd. (2011). Early Islamic institutions: administration and taxation from the Caliphate to the Umayyads and ʿAbbāsids.

Albarrán, J. (2023). This Is Your Miḥrāb: Sacred Spaces and Power in Early Islamic North Africa—Al-Qayrawān as a Case Study. Religions.

Bah, E., Jackson, K., & Potts, D. (2018). Regional Trade institutions in West Africa: Historical Reflections. Journal of International Development, 30, 1255–1272.

Begum, T. (2020). Vernacularization of Islam and Sufism in Medieval Assam: A Study of the Production of Sufi Literature in Local Languages.

Bunza, M., & Karim, L. A. (2021). An Islamic Statecraft in Sub-Saharan Africa: A Study of the Structure and Operations of Governance in the Sokoto Caliphate, Nigeria (1804-1903).

Burke, E. M. (1993). Ira M. Lapidus, A History of Islamic Societies (Cambridge: Cambridge University Press, 1988). Pp. 1002. International Journal of Middle East Studies, 25, 327–330.

Calasso, G. (2021). Constructing the Boundary between Mashriq and Maghrib in Medieval Muslim Sources. The Maghrib in the Mashriq.

Camara, M. S. (2020). The History of Guinea. Oxford Research Encyclopedia of African History.

Campopiano, M. (2017). The End of an Era? The Impact of Early Islamic Expansion on Economic and Social Structures in the Byzantine East. The Journal of European Economic History, 46, 139–150.

Cebeci, A. (2022). Arabic Conquests and Early Islamic Historiography: The Futuh al-Buldan of al-Baladhuri (by Ryan Lynch). American Journal of Islam and Society.

Choueiri, Y. (2005). A companion to the history of the Middle East.

Corisande Fenwick's "Early Islamic North Africa: A New Perspective" (2020).

Crabtree, P. (2008). Encyclopedia of society and culture in the medieval world.

Dampier, G. Y. (2017). The historical influence of the ghazis on the Islamic State. 2, 1–9.

Derbesh, M. (2023). Academic freedom and knowledge tradition of the Arab heritage. HORIZONS A.

Docksai, R. (2014). Book Review: From Arab Spring to Islamic Winter. World Future Review, 6, 215–217.

Fenwick, C. (2020). Early Islamic North Africa: A New Perspective.

Fenwick, C. (2023). Conquest to Conversion. Journal of Islamic Archaeology.

Forde, D. (1943). A Black Byzantium, the Kingdom of Nupe in Nigeria. By S. F. Nadel. 1942. London: Oxford University Press, for the International Institute of African Languages and Cultures. Pp. xvi + 420. Illus., maps. 25s. Africa, 14, 94–96.

Fred M. Donner's "The Early Islamic Conquests" (Princeton University Press, 1981).

Galal-Edeen, G. (2003). Fatimid Cairo: The transformation of an urban logic.

Gómez, M. A. (2019). Prologue. African Dominion.

Gooding, P. (2019). History, Politics, and Culture in Central Tanzania. Oxford Research Encyclopedia of African History.

Huet, D. (2020). The Role of Sufism in Islamic Reform in West Africa. 1.

Ibrahim, A., & Zaria, A. (2017). Sokoto Caliphate scholars and the classical Islamic philosophers: issues in divine command theory of ethics. 87–119.

Ibrahim, M. (1983). Fred M. Donner, The Early Islamic Conquests (Princeton: Princeton University Press, 1981). Pp. xviii + 489. International Journal of Middle East Studies, 15, 577–579.

Joffé, G. (2015). Traditions of governance in North Africa. The Journal of North African Studies, 20, 722–734.

Johnson, D. (1989). The Structure of a Legacy: Military Slavery in Northeast Africa. Ethnohistory, 36, 72–88.

Jonson, T. M. H. (2014). A numismatic history of the early Islamic precious metal coinage of North Africa and the Iberian Peninsula.

Kane, O. (2007). Moderate Revivalists: Islamic Inroads in Sub-Saharan Africa. Harvard International Review, 29, 64.

Kapteijns, L. (2014). The History of Somalia. International Journal of African Historical Studies, 47, 526.

Leguin, C. A. (2004). Reading 1 Trade, Technology, and Culture: The Mali Empire in West Africa Early West African States and the Caravan Trade.

Michael A. Gómez's "African Dominion" (2019) (Gómez, 2019)

Mkacher, A., & Benabbès, M. (2021). Contemporary Historiography on the Beginnings of Islam in North Africa. Revista de Historiografía.

Nickson, T. (2021). Architecture of the Islamic West: North Africa and the Iberian Peninsula, 700–1800. Hispanic Research Journal, 22, 542–544.

Norris, H. (1990). 'Abdulwāḥid Dhanūn Ṭāha: The Muslim conquest and settlement of North Africa and Spain. (Exeter Arabic and Islamic Series.) xiv, 280 pp. London and New York: Routledge, 1989.

Ojha, A. (2016). African women: a historical panorama. Africa Review, 8, 191–193.

Olson, C. (2023). Hendrickson, Jocelyn, Leaving Iberia: Islamic Law and Christian Conquest in North West Africa. Cambridge, MA, Harvard University Press, 2022, 432 pp. Al-Qantara: Revista de Estudios Arabes.

Petry, C. (2022). The Mamluk Sultanate.

Revolution: Structure and Meaning in World History. Said Amir Arjomand, Chicago: University of Chicago Press, 2019. Pp. 400.

Sukdaven, M., & Bagheri, E. (2018). Spreading of Islam without any violence in Central, East and West Africa as a case study. HTS Teologiese Studies/Theological Studies.

Watson, R. (2011). Making Headway: The Introduction of Western Civilization in Colonial Northern Nigeria. The Journal of Imperial and Commonwealth History, 39, 509–512.

Willard, A. (1993). Gold, Islam and Camels: The Transformative Effects of Trade and Ideology. Comparative Civilizations Review, 28, 80–105.

VII

LEGACY AND IMPACT

THE AFTERMATH OF THE ISLAMIC CONQUESTS

The Islamic conquests of Africa brought about significant changes and challenges for the region's indigenous populations. The aftermath of these conquests saw the blending of diverse cultures and the imposition of new religious and social structures. The conquered territories were faced with the need to adapt to the cultural and religious norms of the Islamic rulers, which often resulted in a transformation of the existing societal fabric. The encounter between Islamic conquerors and local populations led to a complex assimilation, assimilation, and cultural exchange process, shaping the region's future trajectory. This chapter delves into the various dimensions of the aftermath of the Islamic conquests, exploring the cultural and religious impacts on indigenous populations and shedding light on the lasting legacies of this pivotal historical period.

CULTURAL AND RELIGIOUS IMPACTS ON INDIGENOUS POPULATIONS

The Islamic conquests brought about significant cultural and religious impacts on the indigenous populations of the conquered territories. The spread of Islam resulted in a transformation of traditional beliefs and practices and the introduction of new customs and rituals. The Arab conquerors often interacted with local populations, leading to a blending of cultures and the emergence of a distinct Islamic-African identity. One of the most notable cultural impacts of the Islamic conquests was the adoption of Arabic as a language of administration, trade, and religion. Arabic script was introduced for writing, leading to the preservation and dissemination of knowledge through written texts. This facilitated the translation and transmission of classical Greek and Roman works and the development of new literary and scholarly traditions. Religiously, the spread of Islam had a profound impact on the indigenous belief systems of North Africa. Many Berber tribes, for example, gradually converted to Islam and integrated Islamic practices into their daily lives. The syncretism of Islamic and traditional African religious practices created a unique and diverse religious landscape in the region.

Furthermore, the construction of mosques and madrasas in conquered territories served as centers for religious education and community gatherings. These institutions played a crucial role in disseminating Islamic teachings and promoting Arabic language and culture. The architecture of these religious buildings also reflected a fusion of Islamic and African design elements, showcasing the artistic and aesthetic exchanges that occurred during this period. In summary, the cultural and religious impacts of the Islamic conquests on indigenous populations were multifaceted and enduring. The blending of traditions, languages, and beliefs created a rich and diverse cultural tapestry that continues to shape the identity of North Africa and beyond.

ECONOMIC CHANGES AND TRADE NETWORKS

Trade networks played a crucial role in the economic changes that resulted from the Islamic conquests in Africa. The expansion of Islam into new territories led to the establishment of extensive trade routes, connecting various regions and facilitating the exchange of goods, ideas, and technologies. These trade networks stimulated economic growth and fostered cultural exchange and the spread of Islamic beliefs. One of the key impacts of the Islamic conquests on trade networks was the integration of existing routes with new ones established by the Muslim rulers. The Islamic caliphates invested heavily in infrastructure, such as roads and bridges, to improve transportation and communication between different regions. This investment encouraged the growth of trade and commerce, leading to the exchange of commodities such as gold, ivory, salt, and slaves across the African continent. The Islamic conquests also brought about changes in the organization of trade. Muslim traders, known as Sahib al-Suq (market owners), played a central role in managing commercial activities in conquered territories. They ensured that trade regulations were enforced, markets were well-supplied, and disputes were resolved fairly. This system of governance promoted stability and trust in trade relationships, attracting merchants from distant lands to participate in the burgeoning markets of the Islamic world.

Furthermore, the spread of Islam along trade routes facilitated cultural exchange and the adoption of new technologies. Muslim scholars and artisans traveled with trade caravans, sharing knowledge and skills in agriculture, architecture, and metallurgy. This cross-cultural exchange enriched local economies and contributed to developing sophisticated urban centers in Africa. Overall, the economic changes brought about by the Islamic conquests had a lasting impact on African trade networks. Integrating diverse regions into a unified economic system, underpinned by Islamic principles of commerce and governance, laid the foundation for the flourishing trade networks that characterized the medieval Islamic world.

SOCIAL AND POLITICAL TRANSFORMATIONS IN CONQUERED TERRITORIES

The social and political landscape of the conquered territories underwent significant transformations in the wake of the Islamic conquests. Integrating diverse populations under the umbrella of the Islamic caliphates led to a complex intermingling of cultures, languages, and societal structures. Indigenous peoples adapted to new ruling systems and governance structures, often reflecting Islamic principles and norms. The emergence of Islamic dynasties and governing bodies brought about a consolidation of power in the conquered regions. Local chieftains and rulers either aligned themselves with the new authorities or faced resistance and suppression. The imposition of Islamic law and administration led to establishing centralized systems that aimed to govern the conquered territories efficiently. Socially, the spread of Islam introduced new cultural practices and norms to the indigenous populations. Adopting Arabic as the language of administration and communication facilitated a sense of unity among diverse ethnic groups. Islamic values such as charity, justice, and compassion influenced social interactions and norms, shaping the everyday lives of the conquered peoples.

Furthermore, the Islamic conquests often brought about a restructuring of social hierarchies and power dynamics. Arab conquerors and settlers often intermarried with local populations, leading to the emergence of new social classes and lineages. The conversion to Islam provided opportunities for social mobility and integration into the ruling elite, while non-Muslim communities maintained their distinct identities and rights under Islamic rule. Politically, the Islamic caliphates established a framework for governance that blended existing administrative practices with Islamic principles. Local administrators were appointed to oversee the conquered territories' day-to-day affairs, ensuring the state apparatus's smooth functioning. Integrating indigenous peoples into the administrative system allowed for autonomy and representation within the broader caliphal structure. Overall, the social and political transformations in the conquered territories reflected the dynamic interplay between Islamic ideals and existing societal norms. The legacy of the Islamic conquests continues to shape these regions' cultural, social, and political landscapes to this day, highlighting the enduring impact of this transformative period in history.

SPREAD OF ISLAMIC ARCHITECTURE AND URBAN PLANNING

The spread of Islamic architecture and urban planning during the Islamic conquests played a significant role in shaping the physical landscape of the conquered territories. Islamic architectural designs and urban planning principles were influenced by a combination of pre-existing local traditions and new ideas brought by the conquerors. Islamic architecture is known for its emphasis on geometric patterns, intricate decorations, and domes and arches. These architectural elements were incorporated into mosques, palaces, madrasas, and other public buildings across the conquered territories. The construction of grand mosques served as places of worship and symbols of Islamic power and culture. Urban planning under Islamic rule often centered around establishing planned cities or expanding and renovating existing settlements. Cities were designed to focus on functionality and organization, with streets laid out in a grid pattern and public spaces designated for markets, mosques, and communal gatherings. Water management systems, such as aqueducts and irrigation channels, were also integrated into urban planning to ensure the efficient distribution of water resources. The influence of Islamic architecture and urban planning extended beyond the physical structures themselves. It profoundly impacted the conquered territories' social and cultural fabric, fostering a sense of unity and identity among the diverse populations. The construction of monumental buildings and cityscapes served as a visual representation of Islamic political and religious authority, reinforcing the ruling elite's ideology.

Furthermore, the spread of Islamic architecture and urban planning facilitated the exchange of ideas and technologies between different regions, synthesizing various artistic traditions. Local artisans and craftsmen adopted and adapted Islamic architectural styles, creating a fusion of artistic expressions reflecting the conquered territories' cultural diversity. In conclusion, the spread of Islamic architecture and urban planning during the Islamic conquests not only transformed the physical environment of the conquered territories but also influenced the social, cultural, and political dynamics of these regions. The legacy of Islamic architectural achievements continues to be celebrated and preserved as a testament to the cultural richness and creativity of the Islamic world.

INFLUENCE ON LANGUAGE AND LITERATURE

The spread of Islamic civilization across Africa significantly influenced language and literature in the region. Arabic, as the Quran and Islamic faith language, became a unifying force in the lands conquered by Islamic caliphates. With its rich vocabulary and complex grammar, the Arabic language served as a vehicle for transmitting knowledge and culture. Islamic scholars and traders were crucial in disseminating Arabic language and literature throughout Africa. They established schools, mosques, and trading posts where Arabic was taught and spoken. This led to the adoption of Arabic as a literary language in many regions, alongside local languages. One of the most notable contributions of Islamic civilization to African literature was the translation of essential works from Greek, Persian, and Indian sources into Arabic. This translation movement, known as the "Golden Age of Islam," helped preserve and transmit classical knowledge to future generations. African scholars and poets also began composing their works in Arabic, blending Islamic themes with indigenous cultural elements. The influence of Arabic literature on Africa can be seen in the development of unique literary genres such as Sufi poetry, historical chronicles, and philosophical treatises. Arabic literary forms, such as the qasida (ode) and the maqama (prose poem), inspired African writers to create distinct styles and expressions.

Furthermore, the Islamic emphasis on education and scholarship established libraries, madrasas, and learning centers across Africa. These institutions became hubs of intellectual exchange, where Arabic language and literature were studied alongside Islamic theology, jurisprudence, and philosophy. As a result of the Islamic conquests, Arabic language and literature became integral components of African cultural identity and heritage. The enduring legacy of Islamic education and scholarship continues to shape the linguistic and literary landscape of the continent, reflecting the enduring impact of Islamic civilization in Africa.

LEGACY OF ISLAMIC EDUCATION AND SCHOLARSHIP

The legacy of Islamic education and scholarship profoundly impacted the regions conquered during the Islamic expansion. Islamic scholars were instrumental in preserving and transmitting knowledge from various civilizations, including Greek, Persian, Indian, and pre-Islamic Arab cultures. The establishment of learning centers such as the House of Wisdom in Baghdad and the Al-Qarawiyyin in Fez served as beacons of intellectual thought. These institutions preserved ancient texts and produced original works that advanced knowledge in fields such as mathematics, astronomy, medicine, philosophy, and theology. Islamic scholars played a pivotal role in translating works from different languages into Arabic, making these texts accessible to a broader audience. This cultural exchange facilitated knowledge transfer across borders and contributed to the flourishing of intellectual inquiry and innovation. Islamic education emphasized the importance of seeking knowledge as a religious duty, and this value system influenced the development of educational institutions and curricula in the conquered territories.

The establishment of madrasas, or Islamic schools, provided a structured environment for learning the Quran, hadith, jurisprudence, and other religious disciplines. The curriculum also included subjects such as mathematics, natural sciences, and philosophy, reflecting the diverse intellectual pursuits embraced by Islamic scholars. Promoting critical thinking and dialectical reasoning encouraged students to engage with ideas from different perspectives, fostering a culture of intellectual curiosity and debate—the legacy of Islamic scholarship extended beyond academia to influence societal norms and values. The emphasis on ethics, morality, and social responsibility in Islamic teachings guided the behavior of scholars and students alike. The concept of Ihsan, or excellence in conduct, underscored the importance of ethical behavior in all aspects of life, including scholarly pursuits. Islamic scholars were not only repositories of knowledge but also exemplars of virtue, humility, and integrity, setting a benchmark for personal and professional conduct. The transmission of knowledge through Islamic education and scholarship had a lasting impact on the conquered territories, shaping these regions' intellectual, cultural, and moral landscape. The legacy of Islamic scholars continues to resonate in modern educational systems, where the principles of critical inquiry, moral rectitude, and intellectual diversity are valued as pillars of a well-rounded education. The enduring influence of Islamic education and scholarship is a testament to the enduring power of knowledge to transcend boundaries and transform societies.

LONG-TERM EFFECTS ON GOVERNANCE AND LEGAL SYSTEMS

The long-term effects of the Islamic conquests on governance and legal systems in the conquered territories were profound and enduring. The establishment of Islamic rule brought about a fundamental transformation in the political and legal structures of the region. Islamic law, known as Sharia, became the basis for the legal system in many of these territories, supplanting existing legal traditions and customs. Under Islamic governance, a system of justice based on equality, justice, and compassion was implemented. Islamic law provided a framework for resolving disputes, enforcing contracts, and ensuring social order. The qadis, or Islamic judges, played a crucial role in interpreting and applying Sharia law through the Quran and Hadith teachings. One of the key innovations introduced by Islamic governance was the concept of the Caliphate, a political institution that combined religious and temporal authority. The Caliphs served as both the spiritual and political leaders of the Muslim community, overseeing the administration of justice and providing governance based on Islamic principles. The Islamic legal system also influenced the development of administrative structures in the conquered territories. Establishing administrative divisions, known as provinces or emirates, helped streamline governance and ensure effective rule. Local administrators appointed by the Caliphs were responsible for managing public affairs, collecting taxes, and maintaining law and order. Over time, the Islamic legal and administrative systems became deeply ingrained in the governance of the conquered territories, shaping their political, social, and economic life. The principles of justice, accountability, and rule of law established by Islamic governance had a lasting impact on the development of these societies, shaping their institutions and governing structures for centuries to come.

INTERACTIONS WITH EXISTING SOCIETIES AND INTEGRATION OF LOCAL CUSTOMS

The interactions between the Islamic conquerors and the existing societies of their conquered regions were complex and multifaceted. Incorporating local customs, traditions, and governing structures played a crucial role in the success of the Islamic conquests in Africa. Rather than imposing a single rigid system, the conquerors often adapted to the local cultures and systems of governance, integrating them into the newly established Islamic rule. Islamic rulers usually retained local leaders and administrators throughout the conquered territories, allowing them to continue governing their regions under the umbrella of Islamic authority. This approach helped maintain stability and order and facilitated the assimilation of diverse cultural practices and traditions into the Islamic framework. One notable aspect of the integration process was incorporating existing legal systems into the newly established Islamic legal framework. Islamic jurists often drew upon local customary laws and judicial practices, integrating them into the broader Islamic legal system. This hybrid legal system allowed for a degree of flexibility and adaptation to local contexts while still upholding Islamic law principles.

Additionally, the Islamic conquerors frequently adopted elements of local languages, customs, and traditions, which helped bridge the cultural divide between the conquerors and the conquered populations. This cultural exchange resulted in a rich tapestry of influences that shaped the social fabric of the conquered territories. Overall, integrating local customs and traditions into the Islamic conquests in Africa was a testament to Islamic rule's pragmatic and adaptive nature. By incorporating existing societal structures and customs, the Islamic conquerors built a lasting foundation for governance that endured long after the initial conquests. This nuanced approach to governance facilitated the spread of Islam and helped foster a sense of unity and mutual understanding among the diverse populations of the conquered territories.

CONTEMPORARY PERSPECTIVES ON THE LEGACY AND SIGNIFICANCE

The legacy of the Islamic conquests in Africa holds significant weight in contemporary perspectives, shaping the cultural landscape and societal norms in the regions impacted by these historical events. Integrating local customs and traditions with Islamic practices has created a rich tapestry of diverse cultural expressions that continue to influence daily life in these areas. One of the key aspects of this legacy is the lasting influence on language and literature. The Arabic language, propagated by the Islamic conquests, remains a prominent language in many African countries, serving as a lingua franca for communication and scholarly pursuits. The literary tradition of Arabic and Islamic texts, including the Quran and other religious writings, has left a profound mark on the literary heritage of these regions, inspiring generations of writers and poets.

Moreover, the impact of Islamic architecture and urban planning is visible in the cities and towns shaped by the conquests. The distinctive architectural styles, characterized by intricate geometric patterns and ornate decorations, showcase the fusion of Islamic aesthetics with local building traditions. From mosques to palaces, these structures stand as a testament to the enduring influence of Islamic culture on the physical environment of Africa. In addition to cultural and architectural influences, the legacy of the Islamic conquests has also left a mark on governance and legal systems in many African countries. The introduction of Islamic law, or Sharia, has shaped the legal frameworks of these nations, influencing matters of family law, property rights, and criminal justice. The principles of justice and equity enshrined in Islamic law continue to guide legal practices and proceedings in these regions. Overall, the contemporary perspectives on the legacy and significance of the Islamic conquests in Africa highlight the ongoing impact of these historical events on the cultural, social, and political fabric of the continent. By recognizing and understanding this legacy, we can gain insights into the complexities of the region's history and appreciate the diverse influences that have shaped its development over the centuries.

REFERENCES

Albarrán, J. (2023). This Is Your Miḥrāb: Sacred Spaces and Power in Early Islamic North Africa—Al-Qayrawān as a Case Study. Religions.(Castiglia, 2022)

Mota, T. (2021). Wolof and Mandinga Muslims in the early Atlantic World: African background, missionary disputes, and social expansion of Islam before the Fula jihads. Atlantic Studies, 20, 150-176. (O'Sullivan et al., 2018)

Campopiano, M. (2017). The End of an Era? The Impact of Early Islamic Expansion on Economic and Social Structures in the Byzantine East. The Journal of European Economic History, 46, 139-150. (Belhaj, 2022)

Frishkopf, M. (2023). Localized Timbres and Tonalities of Qur'ānic Recitation: From Africa to Indonesia. Journal of Islamic and Muslim Studies, 8, 36-57. (Yakunin, 2023)

Castiglia, G. et al. (2021). For an Archaeology of Religious Identity in Adulis (Eritrea) and the Horn of Africa: Sources, Architecture, and Recent Archaeological Excavations. Journal of African Archaeology, 1-32. (Dores, 2024)

Ehinger, J. L. (2015). Religious communities of the Near East from Roman to Islamic rule: sectarianism and identity in an age of transition (5th-8th C). (Larkin & Meyer, 2006)

Larkin, B., & Meyer, B. (2006). Pentecostalism, Islam and culture: New religious movements in West Africa (pp. 286-312).(Gold, 2017)

Bell, D. (2020). The Seat of Drought: Religious Thought and the Sahelian Famine (1968–74) in Mali, West Africa. Mande Studies, 21, 131-152.(Eickelman, 2015)

Frishkopf, M. (2008). "Islamic Music in Africa" as a Tool for African Studies. Canadian Journal of African Studies, 42, 478-507.(Isakhan & Meskell, 2023)

Zakharov, I. (2023). Ethiopia: Reaction of the Religious Landscape to the Change in Religious Policy in the Middle of the 19th – early

21st Centuries. Vostok. Afro-aziatskie obshchestva: istoriia i sovremennost.(Siregar, 2017)

Burlacioiu, C. (2016). Expansion Without Western Mission and Constructing Confessional Identities: The African Orthodox Church between the United States, South Africa and East Africa (1921–1940) (Vol. 6, p. 82).(Naderi & Hassan, 2021)

Matanzima, J. (2022). Exploring the Origins and Expansion of the Nyaminyami (Water Spirit) Belief Systems among the BaTonga People of Northwestern Zimbabwe. Journal of Religion in Africa.(Historical Problems Of Imperial Africa Epdf Download, 2023)

Hackett, R., & Soares, B. (2015). New Media and Religious Transformations in Africa (p. 316).(Castiglia et al., 2021)

Sadouni, S. (2007). New Religious Actors in South Africa: The Example of Islamic Humanitarianism (pp. 103-118).(Rusli & Islam, 2023)

Anizoba, E. (2022). New religious movements and the problem of syncretism: A study of Anioma Healing Ministry, Nawgu, Nigeria. HTS Teologiese Studies/Theological Studies.(Sadouni, 2007)

Maranise, A.M.J. (2012). Investigating the syncretism of Catholicism and voodoo in New Orleans.(Albarrán, 2023)

Sellin, E. (2013). Translingual and Transcultural Patterns in Francophone Literature of the Maghreb (pp. 223-244).(Maranise, 2012)

Barrett, D. B. (1970). Analytical Methods of Studying Religious Expansion in Africa. Journal of Religion in Africa, 3, 22-44.(Selishchev, 2020)

Musoni, P., Machingura, F., & Mamvuto, A. (2020). Religious Artefacts, Practices and Symbols in the Johane Masowe Chishanu yeNyenyedzi Church in Zimbabwe: Interpreting the Visual Narratives (Vol. 46, pp. 1-17).(African Spirituality in the Johane Masowe Chishanu Religious Movement in Zimbabwe: A Christian Church-Sect Dichotomy, 2021)

Further Research

African spirituality in the Johane Masowe Chishanu religious movement in Zimbabwe: A Christian church-sect dichotomy. (2021).

Albarrán, J. (2023). This Is Your Miḥrāb: Sacred Spaces and Power in Early Islamic North Africa—Al-Qayrawān as a Case Study. Religions.

Alkadi, R. (2017). The origin of the Islamic ribbed vaults is famed in North Africa and Spain.

Arıkan, G. (2022). From Pews to Politics: Religious Sermons and Political Participation in Africa By Gwyneth H. McClendon and Rachel Beatty

Riedl. New York, NY: Cambridge University Press, 2019. xii+ 274 pp. 39.99 cloth, 29.99 paper. Politics and Religion, 15, 853–855.

Barrett, D. B. (1970). Analytical Methods of Studying Religious Expansion in Africa. Journal of Religion in Africa, 3, 22–44.

Belhaj, A. (2022). Negotiating the Religious in Contemporary Everyday Life in the 'Islamic World.' Islam and Christian-Muslim Relations, 33, 207–209.

Bell, D. (2020). The Seat of Drought: Religious Thought and the Sahelian Famine (1968–74) in Mali, West Africa. Mande Studies, 21, 131–152.

Bunt, G. (2024). Islamic Algorithms.

Burlacioiu, C. (2016). Expansion Without Western Mission and Constructing Confessional Identities: The African Orthodox Church between the United States, South Africa and East Africa (1921–1940). 6, 82.

Carney, J. J. (2022). The mission of Apolo Kivebulaya. Religious encounter and social change in the Great Lakes, c.1865–1935. By Emma Wild-Wood. (Eastern Africa Series.) Pp. Xviii + 318, incl. 5 ills and 2 maps. Woodbridge: James Currey, 2020. 978 1 84701 246 3. The Journal of Ecclesiastical History, 73, 902–904.

Castiglia, G. (2022). An archaeology of conversion? Evidence from Adulis for early Christianity and religious transition in the Horn of Africa. Antiquity, 96, 1555–1573.

Castiglia, G., Pergola, P., Ciliberti, M., Maletić, B., Pola, M., & Larentis, O. (2021). For an Archaeology of Religious Identity in Adulis (Eritrea) and the Horn of Africa: Sources, Architecture, and Recent Archaeological Excavations. Journal of African Archaeology, 1–32.

Choueiri, Y. (2005). A companion to the history of the Middle East.

Dores, H. G. (2024). Beyond Nation and Empire? Questioning the Role of Religious Missions under Portuguese Colonial Rule at the Turn of the Twentieth Century. Religions.

Douglas, M. (2016). The Effects of Modernization on Religious Change.

Ehinger, J. L. (2015). Religious communities of the Near East from Roman to Islamic rule: sectarianism and identity in an age of transition (5th-8th C).

Eickelman, D. (2015). Who Gets the Past? The Changing Face of Islamic Authority and Religious Knowledge. 135–145.

Fakir, S. (1997). ISLAM, SCIENCE AND RELIGION AND THE CONSTRUCTION OF NEW RELIGIOUS IDENTITIES: A PERSPECTIVE FROM SOUTH AFRICA. 61, 121–128.

Frishkopf, M. (2008). "Islamic Music in Africa" as a Tool for African Studies. Canadian Journal of African Studies / Revue Canadienne Des Études Africaines, 42, 478–507.

Frishkopf, M. (2023). Localized Timbres and Tonalities of Qur'ānic Recitation: From Africa to Indonesia. Journal of Islamic and Muslim Studies, 8, 36–57.

Gaber, T. (2023). Recasting the Religious Architecture of Islam. American Journal of Islam and Society.

Gold, S. (2017). Review of Mara A. Leichtman, Shi'i Cosmopolitanisms in Africa: Lebanese Migration and Religious Conversion in Senegal. Contemporary Islam, 12, 93–95.

Grasso, V. A., Davitashvili, A., & Abuhussein, N. (2023). Introduction. Epigraphy, the Qurʾān, and the Religious Landscape of Arabia. Millennium, 20, 1–14.

Hackett, R., & Soares, B. (2015). New Media and Religious Transformations in Africa. 316.

Khalid, H., Abdalla, W., Abdelgadir, H., Opatz, T., & Efferth, T. (2012). Gems from traditional north-African medicine: medicinal and aromatic plants from Sudan. Natural Products and Bioprospecting, 2, 92–103.

Khalil, H., Bileha, E., & Mortada, H. (2016). Urban Conservation Of The Historic City Of Jugol, Ethiopia: A Syntactic Approach. WIT Transactions on the Built Environment, 159, 149–160.

Larkin, B., & Meyer, B. (2006). Pentecostalism, Islam and culture: New religious movements in West Africa. 286–312.

Maulani, A. (2023). Revealing New Insights: Preserving Islamic Manuscripts in Eastern Indonesia. STUDIA ISLAMIKA.

Mota, T. (2021). Wolof and Mandinga Muslims in the early Atlantic World: African background, missionary disputes, and social expansion of Islam before the Fula jihads. Atlantic Studies, 20, 150–176.

Mouline, N., & Rundell, E. (2014). The Clerics of Islam: Religious Authority and Political Power in Saudi Arabia.

Musoni, P., Machingura, F., & Mamvuto, A. (2020). Religious Artefacts, Practices and Symbols in the Johane Masowe Chishanu yeNyenyedzi Church in Zimbabwe: Interpreting the Visual Narratives. 46, 1–17.

Neubert, D. (2019). A New Framework for the Analysis of Social Structures in Sub-Saharan Africa. Inequality, Socio-Cultural Differentiation and Social Structures in Africa.

Okene, Dr. A. A., & Ahmad, S. (2018). Ibn Khaldun, Cyclical Theory and the Rise and Fall of Sokoto Caliphate, Nigeria West Africa.

O'Sullivan, S., Sajid, M., Agusto, F., Mwangangi, J., Manguvo, A., Wichmann, D., & Kharoshah, M. (2018). Virtual autopsy and community engagement for outbreak response in Africa: traditional, religious and sociocultural perspectives. Egyptian Journal of Forensic Sciences, 8, 1–6.

Robinson, F. (2012). The Islamic World: World System to 'Religious International.' 111–135.

Sadouni, S. (2007). New Religious Actors in South Africa: The Example of Islamic Humanitarianism. 103–118.

Selishchev, N. (2020). The Religious Motivation in Economy as a Factor of Making the New Technological Structure (On the Example of Activity of the Boer's Calvinist Bureaucracy (Part 1). 151–177.

Siregar, S. N. (2017). Nahdlatul Ulama and Its Role in the Development of Islamic Religious Education in Central Tapanuli. Researchers World, 8, 92–103.

Tocqueville, A., & Pitts, J. (2000). Writings on Empire and Slavery..

Xin-hua, X. (2010). On the Native and Foreign Law in the Legal Development in Africa. Journal of Liaoning University.

Yachir, F. (1996). Wither the Arab World. Social Justice, 23, 184.

Online

1. Adam, A. A., & Akanni, A. (2023). Muslim Organizations and Colonialism in Africa.
2. Shumway, R. (2020). Emerging Modernities in 19th Century Africa.
3. Uzoma, R. C. (n.d.). Religious Pluralism, Cultural Differences, and Social Stability in Nigeria.
4. Femi, C. J. (2024). Exploring the Origins of Nigeria's Present-Day Multi-Ethnic, Religious, Socio-Political, and Governmental Dynamics.
5. Hassan Waziry, S. A. E.-F. (2022). Military Architecture and its Impact on the Formation of Islamic Applied Arts.
6. Alamshah, A., & Susmihara. (2023). Religious Transformation In Wajo: The Islamization Era 1582-1626.
7. Rasool, S., & Suleman, M. (2016). Muslim women overcoming marital violence: breaking through 'structural and cultural prisons' created by religious leaders.
8. Aluede, C. O., & Ikhidero, S. I. (2024). Syncretism and Cultural Resilience: The Coexistence and Evolution of Traditional Itolimin and Christian Burial Practices in Esanland, Nigeria.
9. Umar, M., & Mashi, M. (2020). DEMOCRATIZATION PROCESS AND THE UNFOLDING HISTORICAL DIALETICS OF WOMEN POLITICAL PARTICIPATION IN SUB-SAHARAN AFRICA.

10. Okeugo, O. C., Obioha, & Onyinye, J. (2020). African Prose Fiction and the Depiction of Corruption in Islamic Society and Religion: A Critical Study of Abubakar Gimba's Witnesses to Tears and Sacred Apples.

VIII

THE MILITARY STRATEGIES OF THE ISLAMIC CONQUESTS

MILITARY STRATEGIES

The successful conquests of the Islamic armies across Africa were not solely the result of sheer force or numerical superiority. Behind each military campaign lay a meticulously crafted array of strategies that guided the actions of the commanders and soldiers on the battlefield. These military strategies encompassed many factors, ranging from pre-conquest surveys and planning to coordinating different types of forces during battle. By delving into the intricacies of these strategies, we can gain a deeper understanding of the methods employed by the Islamic armies in their quest for expansion and dominance.

PRE-CONQUEST PREPARATION AND PLANNING

Pre-Conquest Preparation and Planning: The success of any military campaign hinges on meticulous preparation and strategic planning. Before embarking on a conquest, Islamic commanders undertook a comprehensive assessment of the target region, including its geographical features, resources, and potential adversaries. This information allowed them to formulate a tailored approach that maximized their strengths and exploited the enemy's weaknesses. Commanders mobilized and trained their troops in the preparatory phase, ensuring they were well-equipped and disciplined for the challenges ahead. Logistics played a crucial role, with supplies and provisions carefully stockpiled and transport routes secured to sustain the advancing forces. Strategic alliances with local tribes or factions were often forged to garner support and intelligence, creating a network of allies that could facilitate the conquest. Diplomatic overtures were also made to potential adversaries to gauge their intentions and sway them to the Islamic cause. In terms of planning, commanders devised flexible strategies that could adapt to changing circumstances on the battlefield. Contingency plans were implemented, and multiple scenarios were considered to anticipate different outcomes. Reconnaissance missions were dispatched to gather real-time information on enemy movements and fortifications, allowing for informed decision-making during the campaign.

Furthermore, commanders paid close attention to the psychological aspect of warfare, employing propaganda and psychological warfare tactics to demoralize the enemy and boost the morale of their troops. Islamic commanders ensured a strong sense of determination and resilience in the face of adversity by instilling a sense of purpose and unity among their forces. Ultimately, the meticulous preparation and strategic planning undertaken before a conquest set the stage for success on the battlefield, laying the groundwork for utilizing cavalry, infantry, and other military strategies to achieve victory.

UTILIZATION OF CAVALRY AND INFANTRY

The successful utilization of cavalry and infantry was pivotal in the Islamic conquests throughout history. Cavalry, consisting of skilled horsemen armed with swords, spears, and bows, provided the mobility and speed necessary to engage enemy forces swiftly. Their agility on the battlefield allowed them to outmaneuver opponents and launch surprise attacks, often disrupting enemy formations and creating chaos. On the other hand, Infantry formed the backbone of the Islamic armies. Well-trained foot soldiers equipped with various weapons like swords, shields, pikes, and infantry units provided stability and strength in key engagements. They often held strategic positions, engaged in close combat, and supported the cavalry units during battles. The coordination between cavalry and infantry units was crucial in achieving military success. Cavalry units often launch rapid assaults to break enemy lines and create openings for infantry units to exploit.

In contrast, infantry units would provide a solid defensive formation to protect the cavalry's flanks and rear during maneuvers.

Moreover, the combination of cavalry charges and infantry advances in synchronized movements allowed Islamic armies to maintain a fluid and dynamic battlefield strategy. This strategic interplay between cavalry and infantry showcased the diversity of tactics employed and highlighted the importance of a well-balanced and coordinated approach to warfare. As Islamic armies expanded their territories, effectively utilizing cavalry and infantry remained a cornerstone of their military strategies. Whether engaging in open-field battles, fortified sieges, or strategic maneuvers, the harmonious coordination between these two essential components of the army ensured the success of the Islamic conquests across various regions and cultures.

SIEGE WARFARE TACTICS

Siege Warfare Tactics play a crucial role in the success of military campaigns throughout history. During the Islamic conquests, strategically using siege tactics was essential in overcoming fortified cities and strongholds. These tactics required meticulous planning, specialized equipment, and skilled manpower. One of the key elements of siege warfare was using siege engines such as catapults, trebuchets, and battering rams. These powerful tools were used to breach defensive walls, towers, and gates, allowing the invading forces to enter the city or fortress.

Additionally, siege towers were constructed to cover soldiers scaling the walls and engage in close combat with defenders. Another essential aspect of siege warfare was establishing supply lines to sustain the besieging forces. The logistics of providing food, water, and ammunition to the troops during a prolonged siege were crucial for maintaining their strength and morale. Often, the success of a siege hinged on the ability to cut off the enemy's supply lines and starve them into submission. Furthermore, psychological warfare played a significant role in siege tactics. Surrounding a city or fortress with a blockade, launching constant attacks, and spreading rumors of impending doom were common strategies to weaken the defenders' resolve. Propaganda, intimidation, and diplomatic negotiations were also employed to convince the besieged to surrender.

In some cases, sieges could last for months or even years, testing the attackers' and defenders' endurance and resilience. The outcome of a siege often depended on military prowess, strategic planning, and sheer determination. Adapting to changing circumstances, innovating new tactics, and exploiting weaknesses in the enemy's defenses were crucial factors in victory in siege warfare. Overall, siege warfare tactics during the Islamic conquests were a complex and multifaceted aspect of military strategy. They required meticulous planning, coordination, and skillful execution to overcome the formidable defenses of fortified cities and strongholds. Victory in siege warfare often meant the difference between success and failure in expanding the Islamic empire across various territories.

USE OF NAVAL FORCES IN CONQUESTS

Naval forces played a crucial role in the success of Islamic conquests, providing strategic advantages and enabling the rapid expansion of territories. The Islamic forces utilized a combination of warships, merchant vessels, and naval tactics to achieve dominance over key maritime regions. By employing a formidable naval presence, they effectively controlled vital trade routes, facilitated communication between conquered territories, and secured coastal areas for further expansion. The use of naval forces also allowed for swift transportation of troops and supplies, enabling the Islamic armies to launch coordinated attacks from sea and land, overwhelming their opponents. These naval strategies not only extended the reach of the Islamic conquests but also ensured the sustainability of their conquests by securing vital maritime resources and preventing enemy reinforcements.

ADAPTATION TO DIFFERENT TERRAINS

One of the key factors that contributed to the success of Islamic conquests was the adaptability of their forces to different terrains. The vast expanse of territories they sought to conquer presented various geographic challenges, from deserts and mountains to forests and rivers. The Islamic armies showcased remarkable flexibility and resourcefulness in maneuvering these diverse landscapes. In arid deserts, where traditional tactics might falter, they utilized their knowledge of desert warfare to their advantage. They excelled in swift raids, utilizing camels for transportation and surprise attacks on enemy outposts. In mountainous regions, where traditional armies might struggle with the rugged terrain, the Islamic forces showcased their ability to navigate through narrow pathways and employ guerrilla tactics to outmaneuver their opponents. They understood the importance of high ground and strategically positioned their forces to gain the upper hand in battles. When faced with dense forests or marshy terrain, the Islamic armies demonstrated adaptability by utilizing light infantry and archers to navigate the challenging landscape. They employed hit-and-run tactics to disrupt enemy movements and maintain the element of surprise.

Moreover, when encountering river crossings or coastal regions, the Islamic forces innovatively employed naval forces to secure strategic waterways and support land-based operations. They understood the significance of controlling maritime routes for transportation and supply lines, effectively integrating naval operations into their military strategy. Overall, the ability of the Islamic armies to adapt to different terrains played a crucial role in their success in conquering diverse regions. Their strategic flexibility and innovative approach to warfare enabled them to overcome geographical obstacles and emerge victorious in various conquests across the vast expanse of Africa and beyond.

COORDINATION AND COMMUNICATION AMONG FORCES

The success of military campaigns during the Islamic Conquests largely depended on the effective coordination and communication among the diverse forces involved. The ability to strategize, relay orders, and maintain cohesive action across vast territories and varied terrains was paramount to achieving victory. Within the ranks of the Islamic armies, a sophisticated communication system was established to ensure seamless coordination during battles. Messengers were dispatched with orders and updates, carrying vital information between commanders and troops. This communication network facilitated quick decision-making and flexibility in response to changing battlefield conditions. Cooperation among military branches, including cavalry, infantry, and siege units, was essential for executing complex maneuvers and tactics. By coordinating their efforts, these diverse forces could leverage their strengths to achieve strategic objectives. This integrated approach allowed for a more unified and effective military campaign.

Furthermore, communication with local populations and allies played a crucial role in the success of the Islamic Conquests. Diplomatic efforts and alliances with indigenous groups helped secure valuable support, resources, and intelligence. By incorporating local allies and understanding the unique dynamics of the regions they were operating in, the

Islamic forces could adapt their strategies and tactics to leverage local knowledge and expertise. The coordination and communication among forces during the Islamic Conquests were instrumental in overcoming geographical and logistical challenges. The Islamic armies achieved military success and established enduring legacies across vast territories by fostering unity, collaboration, and information sharing.

INCORPORATION OF LOCAL ALLIES AND MERCENARIES

Incorporating local allies and mercenaries played a crucial role in the success of the Islamic conquests. By enlisting the support of indigenous populations and hiring skilled fighters from various regions, the expanding Muslim forces could leverage local knowledge, resources, and military expertise to their advantage. These alliances strengthened the Muslim armies and facilitated smoother integration into newly conquered territories. Local allies were often recruited from tribes, clans, or communities sympathetic to the Islamic cause. These alliances were forged through diplomatic negotiations, marriage alliances, and mutual agreements that benefited both parties. By enlisting the support of local tribes and communities, the Muslim armies gained valuable insight into the terrain, local customs, and potential threats in the region. This knowledge was instrumental in planning strategic military campaigns and navigating unfamiliar territories. Mercenaries, on the other hand, were hired soldiers who fought for financial gain or other rewards. These skilled fighters brought a wealth of military experience and expertise to the Islamic armies, supplementing their forces with specialized combat skills. Mercenaries were often employed to bolster the strength of the Muslim armies, especially in battles that required specific tactical abilities or specialized training. Recruiting local allies and mercenaries was a strategic maneuver that allowed Muslim forces to adapt to diverse environments and combat situations. By incorporating fighters from different backgrounds and regions, the Islamic armies could field a more varied and versatile fighting force. This diversity contributed to their success in engaging with various adversaries and overcoming multiple challenges on the battlefield.

In conclusion, incorporating local allies and mercenaries was key to the military strategies employed during the Islamic conquests. By forging alliances with indigenous populations and hiring skilled fighters from different regions, the Muslim forces strengthened their armies, gained valuable local knowledge, and adapted to the ever-changing dynamics of warfare. These alliances and mercenary arrangements played a vital role in the success of the Islamic conquests and contributed to the establishment of a vast and enduring empire.

FLEXIBILITY AND INNOVATION IN MILITARY APPROACHES

During the Islamic conquests, flexibility and innovation played crucial roles in the success of military approaches. Adapting to changing circumstances, utilizing diverse strategies, and innovating in response to challenges were key factors in achieving victory on the battlefield. Muslim commanders demonstrated remarkable flexibility in their military tactics, often adjusting their approach based on the terrain, enemy tactics, and available resources. One of how Islamic forces showed flexibility was in their use of combined arms tactics. By utilizing a mix of cavalry, infantry, archers, and siege engines, Muslim armies could respond effectively to various threats and challenges. This versatility allowed them to engage in multiple military operations, from fast-paced raids to prolonged sieges. In addition, Islamic commanders displayed a willingness to experiment with new tactics and strategies. They were not bound by tradition or rigid military doctrines but instead sought to adapt their approach to their specific circumstances. This spirit of innovation allowed Muslim forces to surprise their enemies and gain a strategic advantage on the battlefield.

Furthermore, the Islamic conquests blended military traditions from different cultures and regions. Muslim armies drew on diverse groups' expertise, incorporating local allies' and mercenaries' knowledge and skills into their military strategies. This cross-cultural exchange enriched their military capabilities and enabled them to combine the best practices from various traditions. The legacy of the flexibility and innovation displayed by Islamic forces during the conquests continues to influence military thinking. Adapting quickly to changing conditions, thinking creatively about tactics and strategies, and integrating diverse perspectives remain essential for success on the battlefield. By studying the military approaches of the Islamic conquests, modern military leaders can gain valuable insights into the power of flexibility and innovation in achieving victory in conflict.

LEGACY OF MILITARY STRATEGIES IN ISLAMIC CONQUESTS

The legacy of the military strategies employed during the Islamic conquests in Africa is a testament to the effectiveness and adaptability of the Islamic armies. These conquests not only resulted in the expansion of Islamic territories but also left a lasting impact on military tactics and approaches in the region. The innovative use of cavalry and infantry in coordinated attacks allowed the Islamic forces to maneuver and overwhelm their opponents swiftly. This dynamic approach to warfare laid the foundation for future military operations and strategies in the region. The successful integration of siege warfare tactics, such as using catapults and other siege engines, showcased the strategic thinking and resourcefulness of the Islamic armies. These methods were instrumental in capturing fortified enemy strongholds and cities, demonstrating the importance of adaptability and creativity in military campaigns. Naval forces played a crucial role in the Islamic conquests, enabling the rapid mobilization of troops and resources across the vast coastal regions of Africa. The strategic utilization of naval power allowed the Islamic forces to control key maritime trade routes and establish dominance over rival naval powers. The ability to adapt to different terrains, whether traversing arid deserts or navigating dense forests, highlighted the versatility and resilience of the Islamic armies. This adaptability ensured that the conquests could continue unhindered, regardless of the challenging environmental conditions they faced. The coordination and communication among the various branches of the military and the effective utilization of local allies and mercenaries further reinforced the success of the Islamic conquests in Africa. This collaborative approach was essential in maintaining unity of purpose and maximizing military effectiveness on the battlefield. The legacy of the military strategies employed during the Islamic conquests continues to influence military thinking in the region today. The lessons learned from these conquests, in terms of flexibility, innovation, and strategic thinking, serve as a reminder of the enduring impact of these historic campaigns on the art of war.

REFERENCES

English :

1. Kennedy, Hugh. (2007). The Great Arab Conquests: How the Spread of Islam Changed the World We Live In. Philadelphia: Da Capo Press.
2. Nicolle, David. (2009). Armies of the Muslim Conquest. Oxford: Osprey Publishing.
3. Kaegi, Walter Emil. (2010). Muslim Expansion and Byzantine Collapse in North Africa. Cambridge: Cambridge University Press.
4. Donner, Fred M. (1981). The Early Islamic Conquests. Princeton: Princeton University Press.
5. Nicolle, David. (2014). Armies of the Caliphates 862-1098. Oxford: Osprey Publishing.
6. Wheatcroft, Andrew. (2003). Infidels: A History of the Conflict Between Christendom and Islam. New York: Random House.
7. Hill, D.R. (1993). Islamic Science and Engineering. Edinburgh: Edinburgh University Press.
8. Akram, A.I. (2009). The Sword of Allah: Khalid bin Al-Waleed, His Life and Campaigns. Birmingham: Maktabah Publishers.

Arabic :

1. الطبري، محمد بن جرير. (1967). تاريخ الرسل والملوك. القاهرة: دار المعارف. (Al-Tabari, Muhammad ibn Jarir. (1967). Tarikh al-Rusul wa-l-Muluk. Cairo: Dar al-Ma'arif.)
2. ابن الأثير، علي بن محمد. (1987). الكامل في التاريخ. بيروت: دار الكتب العلمية. (Ibn al-Athir, Ali ibn Muhammad. (1987). Al-Kamil fi al-Tarikh. Beirut: Dar al-Kutub al-'Ilmiyya.)

3. البلاذري، أحمد بن يحيى. (1988). فتوح البلدان. بيروت: دار ومكتبة الهلال. (Al-Baladhuri, Ahmad ibn Yahya. (1988). Futuh al-Buldan. Beirut: Dar wa Maktabat al-Hilal.)
4. ابن عبد الحكم، عبد الرحمن. (1964). فتوح مصر والمغرب. القاهرة: مكتبة الثقافة الدينية. (Ibn 'Abd al-Hakam, 'Abd al-Rahman. (1964). Futuh Misr wa-l-Maghrib. Cairo: Maktabat al-Thaqafah al-Diniyya.)
5. الواقدي، محمد بن عمر. (1984). فتوح الشام. بيروت: دار الجيل. (Al-Waqidi, Muhammad ibn 'Umar. (1984). Futuh al-Sham. Beirut: Dar al-Jil.)

French :

1. Djaït, Hichem. (2007). La Grande Discorde: Religion et politique dans l'Islam des origines. Paris: Gallimard.
2. Micheau, Françoise. (2012). Les débuts de l'Islam: Jalons pour une nouvelle histoire. Paris: Téraèdre.
3. Blankinship, Khalid Yahya. (2018). Guerres et conquêtes du premier Islam. Paris: Editions du Rocher.
4. Borrut, Antoine. (2011). Entre mémoire et pouvoir: L'espace syrien sous les derniers Omeyyades et les premiers Abbassides. Leiden: Brill.
5. Picard, Christophe. (2000). Le monde musulman du XIe au XVe siècle. Paris: SEDES.
6. Cahen, Claude. (1982). L'Islam: Des origines au début de l'Empire ottoman. Paris: Hachette.
7. Mantran, Robert. (1986). L'expansion musulmane (VIIe-XIe siècles). Paris: Presses Universitaires de France.

IX

THE ROLE OF KEY FIGURES IN THE CONQUESTS

KEY FIGURES

Throughout history, key figures have played pivotal roles in shaping the course of conquests and revolutions. These individuals possess exceptional leadership qualities, strategic acumen, and unwavering determination that propel them to the forefront of significant historical events. They are often revered for their vision, courage, and ability to inspire and lead others in times of uncertainty and adversity. In the context of the Islamic conquests, these key figures emerged as formidable leaders who left an indelible mark on the region's history.

THE LEADERSHIP OF KHALID IBN AL-WALID

Khalid ibn al-Walid, also known as the "Sword of Allah," was a key figure in the Islamic conquests, renowned for his exceptional leadership on the battlefield. His strategic brilliance and military prowess earned him a reputation as one of the greatest tacticians of his time. Khalid's leadership was characterized by his fearlessness, determination, and unwavering commitment to the cause of Islam. Khalid led his troops with unmatched skill and agility and secured several crucial victories for the Islamic forces. His innovative tactics and decisive actions often turned the tide of battle in favor of the Muslims. Known for his swift and decisive maneuvers, Khalid's ability to anticipate and exploit his enemy's weaknesses set him apart as a master tactician. Despite facing overwhelming odds and formidable opponents, Khalid's leadership inspired unwavering loyalty and devotion among his troops. His calm demeanor and strategic acumen instilled confidence in his soldiers, enabling them to conquer seemingly impossible challenges successfully. Khalid's strategic vision and ability to adapt to changing circumstances were instrumental in rapidly expanding Islamic territories. Khalid ibn al-Walid's legacy endures as a testament to his exceptional leadership and military prowess. His unparalleled contributions to the Islamic conquests have cemented his place in history as a legendary figure whose feats continue to inspire admiration and respect.

THE INFLUENCE OF AMR IBN AL-AS

Amr ibn al-As, a prominent figure in the Islamic conquests, played a significant role in shaping the expansion of the Islamic empire. Known for his strategic prowess and diplomatic skills, Amr ibn al-As was a key commander who led successful campaigns across Egypt and North Africa. Amr's military expertise and leadership were instrumental in the conquest of Egypt, a pivotal region in the expansion of the Islamic empire. His tactical understanding and ability to adapt to varying battlefield conditions enabled him to achieve decisive victories and secure strategic strongholds in the region. In addition to his military achievements, Amr ibn al-As was also revered for his diplomatic finesse. He skillfully navigated complex political landscapes, forging alliances with local tribes and winning the support of indigenous populations. His ability to establish effective communication channels and foster alliances proved crucial in consolidating conquests and maintaining stability in newly acquired territories. Amr's legacy extends beyond his military conquests, as he was also known for his administrative skills and governance abilities. He implemented efficient administrative systems, promoted economic development, and fostered cultural exchange within the conquered territories. His visionary leadership laid the foundation for long-term stability and prosperity in the regions under his command. Overall, the influence of Amr ibn al-As in the Islamic conquests cannot be overstated. His strategic brilliance, diplomatic acumen, and administrative prowess were instrumental in expanding the Islamic empire and shaping its legacy in the conquered territories.

CONTRIBUTIONS OF UMAR IBN AL-KHATTAB

Umar ibn al-Khattab, often called Umar the Great, played a pivotal role in the Islamic conquests through his leadership, strategic vision, and administrative abilities. As the second Caliph of the Rashidun Caliphate, Umar's contributions were instrumental in shaping the expansion of the Islamic Empire. Umar's most notable achievement was establishing a highly efficient administrative system that helped govern the vast territories under Islamic rule. He divided the empire into provinces, each governed by a capable administrator responsible for ensuring justice, security, and proper governance. This decentralized system allowed for effective administration and swift decision-making, stabilizing the empire. Umar's military strategies were characterized by their pragmatism and effectiveness. He carefully selected competent military commanders and devised strategic plans that capitalized on his forces' strengths while exploiting his adversaries' weaknesses. Under his leadership, the Islamic armies achieved significant victories against powerful empires such as the Byzantines and the Sassanids, expanding the boundaries of the Islamic Empire.

Furthermore, Umar's commitment to justice and equality left a lasting legacy in the conquered territories. He implemented reforms to protect the rights of non-Muslims living under Islamic rule, promoting tolerance and coexistence among diverse communities. Umar's emphasis on social justice and welfare policies endeared him to Muslims and non-Muslims, fostering unity and solidarity within the empire. Umar's leadership during the Islamic conquests was marked by wisdom, courage, and a deep duty to his people. His contributions facilitated the rapid expansion of the Islamic Empire and laid the foundations for a just and prosperous society. Umar ibn al-Khattab's enduring legacy as a visionary statesman and military leader inspires generations of leaders and scholars today.

STRATEGIC BRILLIANCE OF SALAH AD-DIN

Salah ad-Din, also known as Saladin, emerged as a strategic genius during the Islamic conquests, particularly as a military leader. He was instrumental in the reclamation of Jerusalem during the Crusades and demonstrated remarkable foresight and tactical acumen throughout his campaigns. Salah ad-Din's military brilliance was exemplified by his ability to adapt to changing circumstances on the battlefield. He was known for his careful planning, meticulous attention to detail, and swift decision-making during times of crisis. His leadership style inspired loyalty and dedication among his troops, fostering a sense of unity and purpose that contributed to his success on the battlefield. One of Salah ad-Din's most notable achievements was the recapture of Jerusalem in 1187. Through military strategy, diplomacy, and perseverance, he defeated the Crusader forces and reclaimed the holy city for the Muslims. His compassion and chivalry towards his enemies and his respect for religious diversity earned him a reputation as a noble and honorable leader. Salah ad-Din's strategic brilliance extended beyond the battlefield. He was also adept at administration, diplomacy, and statecraft, ensuring the stability and prosperity of his realm. His commitment to justice, fairness, and good governance set him apart as a leader who cared deeply for the well-being of his people. In conclusion, Salah ad-Din's strategic brilliance was crucial in shaping history during the Islamic conquests. His military prowess, leadership skills, and commitment to justice left a lasting legacy that inspires admiration and respect today.

LEGACY OF TARIQ IBN ZIYAD

Tariq ibn Ziyad's legacy is etched in the annals of history as a testament to his military prowess and strategic insight. His pivotal role in the Islamic conquest of the Iberian Peninsula in 711 AD laid the foundation for establishing Muslim rule in Spain. Tariq, a Berber general under the command of Musa ibn Nusayr, led the daring invasion of the Visigothic kingdom, crossing the Strait of Gibraltar with a comparatively small army of predominantly Berber and Arab soldiers. Tariq's audacious military strategy and leadership skills were instrumental in securing a series of decisive victories against the Visigothic forces, culminating in the defeat of King Roderic at the Battle of Guadalete. His ability to inspire and motivate his troops and his tactical brilliance on the battlefield facilitated the swift conquest of key cities such as Toledo, Cordoba, and Sevilla. Beyond his military achievements, Tariq ibn Ziyad is revered for his fair and just governance of the newly conquered territories. He implemented policies promoting religious tolerance and economic prosperity, earning the respect and loyalty of Muslim and non-Muslim populations. Tariq's administration laid the groundwork for the cultural exchange and intellectual flourishing that characterized the era of Al-Andalus. Despite the eventual recall of Tariq by the Umayyad Caliphate, his legacy endured in the collective memory of the Iberian Peninsula. In honor of the legendary general, the iconic Rock of Gibraltar, known as Jebel Tariq (Mountain of Tariq), stands as a symbolic reminder of his enduring impact on the region. Tariq ibn Ziyad's legacy as a visionary military leader, benevolent administrator, and cultural bridge-builder continues to inspire generations to this day, underscoring his enduring importance in the annals of history.

THE DIPLOMACY OF ABD AL-RAHMAN I

Abd al-Rahman I was a distinguished leader known for his diplomatic prowess during the Islamic conquests. His ability to navigate complex political situations and forge alliances played a crucial role in the success of the Muslim expansion into new territories. Abd al-Rahman I was a master of diplomacy, adept at building strategic relationships with local leaders and tribes to further the goals of the Islamic conquests. One of Abd al-Rahman I's key strategies was establishing alliances with indigenous populations, earning their loyalty and support. By understanding the cultural and political dynamics of the regions he sought to conquer, Abd al-Rahman I could leverage existing power structures to his advantage. He recognized the importance of collaboration and cooperation in achieving lasting success in newly conquered territories. Abd al-Rahman I also demonstrated a keen understanding of the importance of negotiation and compromise in diplomacy. Instead of relying solely on military force, he sought peaceful resolutions through dialogue and mediation whenever possible. This approach helped minimize conflict and contributed to the long-term stability of the regions under his control.

Additionally, Abd al-Rahman I was skilled at managing diverse groups and fostering unity among different factions. He bridged cultural and religious divides, fostering a sense of common purpose among his followers. By promoting inclusivity and tolerance, Abd al-Rahman I secured the loyalty of people from various backgrounds, strengthening the overall strength of the Muslim forces. Overall, Abd al-Rahman I's diplomatic acumen proved instrumental in the Islamic conquests, laying the groundwork for successfully expanding and consolidating Muslim rule in new territories. His strategic alliances and commitment to peaceful resolution set a precedent for future leaders, illustrating the power of diplomacy in achieving military and political objectives. Abd al-Rahman I's legacy as a skillful diplomat endures as a testament to his enduring contribution to the history of the Islamic conquests.

MILITARY PROWESS OF UQBA IBN NAFI

Uqba ibn Nafi, a military commander renowned for his strategic insight and battlefield prowess, played a crucial role in the Islamic conquests of North Africa. Born in Mecca, Uqba's military career was marked by numerous successful campaigns and conquests, earning him a distinguished reputation among his peers and adversaries alike. Uqba's military prowess was exemplified in his leadership during the conquest of North

Africa, where he skillfully led the Muslim forces to victory in numerous battles against the Berber tribes and Byzantine forces. His strategic insights and tactical brilliance were instrumental in securing key territories and establishing Muslim dominance in the region. Known for his bold and daring military strategies, Uqba was unrelenting in his pursuit of victory. He demonstrated exceptional skill in maneuvering his troops on the battlefield, exploiting his enemies' weaknesses, and launching decisive attacks that ensured the success of his campaigns. Uqba's leadership on the battlefield inspired loyalty and admiration among his soldiers, who trusted in his abilities to lead them to victory. His charisma and courage under fire instilled confidence in his troops and motivated them to fight with unwavering determination and resilience. Beyond his military achievements, Uqba was also known for his compassion and fairness towards those under his command. He treated both allies and enemies with respect, earning him the reputation of a noble and virtuous leader who upheld the principles of justice and integrity on the battlefield. In conclusion, Uqba ibn Nafi's military prowess and leadership were instrumental in the success of the Islamic conquests in North Africa. His strategic brilliance, bold tactics, and unwavering commitment to victory secured key victories and established a lasting legacy in the annals of Islamic military history.

ADMINISTRATIVE SKILLS OF MUSA IBN NUSAYR

Musa ibn Nusayr was a skilled administrator whose contributions played a crucial role in the success of the Islamic conquests in Africa. Known for his strategic planning and organizational abilities, Musa was appointed as the governor of Ifriqiya by the Umayyad Caliphate. Under his leadership, the region experienced significant growth and development.

Musa implemented effective policies to govern the newly conquered territories, focusing on establishing law and order, promoting economic prosperity, and fostering cultural exchange. He was known for his fair and just governance, earning the respect and loyalty of the local population. One of Musa's key achievements was establishing a well-structured administrative system that facilitated efficient governance and resource management. He appointed capable officials to oversee different aspects of administration, including finance, justice, and infrastructure development. Musa also played a pivotal role in promoting religious tolerance and fostering harmony among the diverse communities in the conquered territories. His inclusive approach and respect for the local customs and traditions helped maintain social stability and peace. Overall, Musa ibn Nusayr's administrative skills were instrumental in ensuring the smooth and successful integration of the newly conquered territories into the Islamic empire. His legacy as a capable and visionary administrator continues to be admired and studied to this day.

CONCLUSION ON THE SIGNIFICANCE OF KEY FIGURES IN THE CONQUESTS

Musa ibn Nusayr's remarkable administrative skills played a crucial role in the success of the Islamic conquests in Africa. His ability to efficiently organize resources, establish governance structures, and maintain stability in newly conquered territories set a standard for future generations of leaders. By implementing fair and just policies, promoting economic development, and fostering cultural exchange, Musa ibn Nusayr contributed significantly to the long-term viability of the Islamic empire in Africa. His legacy continues to inspire leaders to prioritize effective administration as a key component of conquest and governance.

REFERENCES

Arabic:

ابن كثير، إسماعيل بن عمر. (1988). البداية والنهاية. بيروت: دار إحياء التراث العربي. (Ibn Kathir, Ismail ibn Umar. (1988). Al-Bidaya wa-l-Nihaya. Beirut: Dar Ihya al-Turath al-Arabi.)

ابن الأثير، علي بن محمد. (1987). الكامل في التاريخ. بيروت: دار الكتب العلمية. (Ibn al-Athir, Ali ibn Muhammad. (1987). Al-Kamil fi al-Tarikh. Beirut: Dar al-Kutub al-'Ilmiyya.)

ابن خلدون، عبد الرحمن. (2004). تاريخ ابن خلدون. بيروت: دار الفكر. (Ibn Khaldun, Abd al-Rahman. (2004). Tarikh Ibn Khaldun. Beirut: Dar al-Fikr.)

المقري، أحمد بن محمد. (1968). نفح الطيب من غصن الأندلس الرطيب. بيروت: دار صادر. (Al-Maqqari, Ahmad ibn Muhammad. (1968). Nafh al-Tib min Ghusn al-Andalus al-Ratib. Beirut: Dar Sadir.)

ابن عبد الحكم، عبد الرحمن. (1964). فتوح مصر والمغرب. القاهرة: مكتبة الثقافة الدينية. (Ibn 'Abd al-Hakam, 'Abd al-Rahman. (1964). Futuh Misr wa-l-Maghrib. Cairo: Maktabat al-Thaqafah al-Diniyya.)

English :

Akram, A.I. (2009). The Sword of Allah: Khalid bin Al-Waleed, His Life and Campaigns. Birmingham: Maktabah Publishers.

Kennedy, Hugh. (2007). The Great Arab Conquests: How the Spread of Islam Changed the World We Live In. Philadelphia: Da Capo Press.

Gabrieli, Francesco. (2010). Arab Historians of the Crusades. London: Routledge.

Lane-Poole, Stanley. (2002). Saladin and the Fall of the Kingdom of Jerusalem. New York: Cosimo Classics.

Collins, Roger. (1989). The Arab Conquest of Spain, 710-797. Oxford: Blackwell.

Hrbek, Ivan. (1992). Africa from the Seventh to the Eleventh Century. Berkeley: University of California Press.

Humphreys, R. Stephen. (1977). From Saladin to the Mongols: The Ayyubids of Damascus, 1193-1260. Albany: State University of New York Press.

Bennison, Amira K. (2016). The Almoravid and Almohad Empires. Edinburgh: Edinburgh University Press.

French:

Micheau, Françoise. (2012). Les débuts de l'Islam: Jalons pour une nouvelle histoire. Paris: Téraèdre.

Djaït, Hichem. (2007). La Grande Discorde: Religion et politique dans l'Islam des origines. Paris: Gallimard.

Eddé, Anne-Marie. (2008). Saladin. Paris: Flammarion.

Sénac, Philippe. (2010). Le Monde musulman: Des origines au XIe siècle. Paris: Armand Colin.

Guichard, Pierre. (2000). Al-Andalus: 711-1492. Paris: Hachette.

Mouton, Jean-Michel. (2009). Saladin, le sultan chevalier. Paris: Gallimard.

Fierro, Maribel. (2005). Abd al-Rahman III: Le premier calife de Cordoue. Paris: Sindbad.

X

REFLECTIONS ON THE ISLAMIC CONQUESTS IN AFRICA

THE ISLAMIC CONQUESTS IN AFRICA

Amidst the vast and diverse landscape of Africa, the Islamic conquests marked a pivotal era of transformation and evolution. As the powerful forces of Islam expanded across the continent, they brought with them an array of sociopolitical changes that would shape the course of history for generations to come. The arrival of Islamic conquests in Africa ushered in a new era of governance and administration. The conquered territories saw the establishment of Islamic caliphates and emirates, which introduced a system of governance based on Islamic law. This new political order not only influenced the legal framework of these regions but also laid the foundation for the integration of Islamic principles into the social fabric of African societies. The sociopolitical impact of the Islamic conquests was not limited to governance alone. These conquests also facilitated cultural exchange and interaction between diverse ethnic groups. The spread of Islam enabled the creation of a shared identity among various communities, leading to a sense of unity and solidarity that transcended traditional tribal boundaries. This cultural assimilation played a crucial role in fostering a sense of collective identity among the inhabitants of the conquered territories. Furthermore, the Islamic conquests brought about significant changes in the economic landscape of Africa. The establishment of trade routes and commercial networks facilitated the exchange of goods and ideas between different regions. The introduction of Islamic economic principles, such as the prohibition of usury and promotion of fair trade, contributed to the development of a more equitable and prosperous economy in these regions. In addition to the political and economic transformations, the Islamic conquests also had a profound impact on the religious landscape of Africa. The spread of Islam resulted in the conversion of a significant portion of the population to the new faith, leading to the establishment of vibrant Muslim communities across the continent. This religious transformation not only influenced the spiritual beliefs of the people but also shaped their cultural practices and traditions. Overall, the introduction of the Islamic conquests in Africa heralded a period of profound change and innovation. The sociopolitical impact of these conquests was far-reaching, laying the groundwork for the cultural, economic, and religious transformations that would define the region for centuries to come.

SOCIOPOLITICAL IMPACT OF THE CONQUESTS

The Islamic conquests in Africa brought about significant sociopolitical changes across the region. One of the key impacts was the establishment of new political structures, as Islamic rulers introduced systems of governance based on Islamic principles. This led to the creation of emirates and caliphates, which replaced traditional African kingdoms and chieftaincies. The Islamic rulers implemented Sharia law, which influenced legal systems and social norms within these societies. Additionally, the Islamic conquests facilitated the spread of Arabic language and script, becoming languages of administration and education in many regions. Trade routes were expanded, connecting Africa with other parts of the Islamic world and facilitating the exchange of goods and ideas. Furthermore, the Islamic conquests led to the integration of African societies into the wider Islamic caliphate, fostering cultural exchange and religious syncretism. The sociopolitical impact of the Islamic conquests in Africa was profound, shaping the political landscape and cultural fabric of the region for centuries to come.

CULTURAL INFLUENCE AND EXCHANGE

The Islamic conquests in Africa brought about significant cultural influence and exchange between the Arab conquerors and the indigenous African populations. This exchange of ideas, beliefs, and practices resulted in a rich tapestry of cultural diversity that laid the foundation for the development of new artistic, architectural, linguistic, and culinary traditions in the region. Additionally, the spread of Islam through these conquests played a crucial role in shaping the cultural landscape of Africa, as local customs and traditions intertwined with those of the Arab conquerors to create a unique cultural fusion that continues to define the region to this day. The blending of Arab and African cultures not only enriched the artistic and intellectual life of the region but also fostered a spirit of tolerance and coexistence among different ethnic and religious communities. Through trade, travel, and intermarriage, the cultural interchange between Arabs and Africans flourished, bringing about a shared heritage that transcended ethnic and religious boundaries. This cultural exchange not only enriched the lives of those living in the conquered territories but also had a lasting impact on the broader Islamic world, as African influences found their way into the art, literature, music, and architecture of the wider Muslim community. The legacy of this cultural exchange can still be seen in the vibrant bazaars of North Africa, the intricate mosques of the Horn of Africa, and the diverse cuisines of the Maghreb, serving as a testament to the enduring impact of the Islamic conquests on the cultural landscape of Africa.

ECONOMIC CONSEQUENCES OF THE CONQUESTS

The Islamic conquests in Africa had far-reaching economic consequences that reshaped trade networks, established new markets, and influenced the production and distribution of goods. One of the key economic impacts of the conquests was the integration of African regions into the larger Islamic commercial networks, facilitating trade and exchange of goods across vast distances. The expansion of Islamic rule brought stability and security to trade routes, encouraging merchants to travel freely and conduct business without fear of banditry or political instability. Furthermore, the Islamic conquests introduced new agricultural techniques and crops to African societies, leading to increased productivity and agricultural innovation. The adoption of Islamic fiscal policies and administrative practices also allowed for more efficient resource management and tax collection, which in turn stimulated economic growth and development in conquered territories. The conquests also spurred the growth of urban centers and the establishment of commercial hubs that served as important centers of trade and commerce. Markets flourished, attracting merchants from different regions and fostering cultural exchange and diversity. The wealth generated from trade and economic activities fueled the construction of impressive architectural projects, such as mosques, palaces, and other public works, showcasing the prosperity and sophistication of Islamic societies in Africa. Additionally, the conquests played a significant role in the development of Islamic banking and financial systems, which facilitated the flow of capital and investment across various regions. The introduction of standardized currency and financial instruments promoted economic stability and encouraged long-term investment in infrastructure projects and commercial ventures. Overall, the economic consequences of the Islamic conquests in Africa were multifaceted, influencing trade, agriculture, urban development, and financial systems. The integration of African regions into the larger Islamic economic networks fostered growth and prosperity, laying the foundation for vibrant and dynamic economies that thrived under Islamic rule.

RELIGIOUS TRANSFORMATION IN AFRICAN SOCIETIES

Religious Transformation in African Societies The Islamic conquests in Africa brought about significant religious transformations in the region. With the spread of Islam through military campaigns and trade networks, African societies witnessed a shift in religious practices and beliefs. Many indigenous African communities embraced Islam, either voluntarily or under duress, leading to the coexistence of multiple faiths within the same region. The introduction of Islam introduced new religious practices, rituals, and beliefs to African societies. The monotheistic nature of Islam resonated with some communities, while others integrated Islamic teachings with their existing spiritual traditions. As a result, syncretic forms of worship emerged, blending elements of Islam with indigenous beliefs. Islamic conquests also led to the establishment of mosques, madrasas (educational institutions), and religious centers throughout Africa. These institutions served as hubs for religious education, community gatherings, and social welfare activities, contributing to the dissemination of Islamic teachings and values. The spread of Islam in Africa also influenced cultural practices and societal norms. Islamic principles of social justice, charity, and equality gained prominence in African societies, shaping their ethical framework and governance systems. The concept of ummah, or community of believers, promoted solidarity and cohesion among diverse ethnic and religious groups within the Islamic world. Despite the widespread acceptance of Islam, resistance to conversion and religious syncretism also occurred in some parts of Africa. Indigenous religious leaders and communities often resisted the imposition of Islamic rule and sought to preserve their traditional beliefs and practices. The presence of local spiritual leaders and the continued observance of indigenous rituals reflected the complexities of religious transformation in Africa. Overall, the religious transformation brought about by the Islamic conquests in Africa was a dynamic and multifaceted process. It resulted in the coexistence of diverse religious traditions, the emergence of syncretic practices, and the integration of Islamic principles into African societies. This intersection of religious beliefs and practices continues to shape the cultural landscape of the continent, highlighting the enduring legacy of the Islamic conquests in Africa.

RESISTANCE AND REVOLTS AGAINST ISLAMIC CONQUESTS

Resistance and revolts against Islamic conquests were not uncommon in African societies during this period, as various local rulers and communities fiercely opposed the expansion of Islamic influence. Many of these resistance movements were driven by a desire to preserve existing cultural and religious traditions, as well as by a reluctance to submit to foreign rule. These revolts often took the form of armed uprisings and rebellions, with local leaders rallying their followers to resist the encroachment of Islamic forces. Some resistance movements were short-lived and isolated, while others persisted for years and posed a significant challenge to the advance of the Islamic conquests. One notable example of resistance against Islamic conquests was the Berber revolt led by Kahina in North Africa. Kahina, a Berber queen and military leader, fiercely resisted the Arab Muslim forces that were trying to conquer the region. Her guerilla tactics and strategic alliances with other local tribes prolonged the conflict and made the conquest of North Africa a difficult and costly endeavor for the Islamic forces. In other regions of Africa, such as in the Horn of Africa, resistance to Islamic conquests also took hold. Local rulers and communities put up a fierce fight against the advancing Islamic armies, determined to defend their autonomy and independence. These resistance movements often drew on a deep sense of identity and cultural pride, motivating people to stand up against outside forces. Despite the challenges posed by these resistance movements, the Islamic conquests eventually succeeded in establishing a lasting presence in many parts of Africa. However, the legacy of these revolts and uprisings remains a reminder of the complex and often violent interactions between different cultures and civilizations during this transformative period of history.

HISTORICAL PERSPECTIVES ON THE CONQUESTS

Historical Perspectives on the Conquests Scholars have long debated the significance and impact of the Islamic conquests in Africa. These conquests were not isolated events but rather part of a larger historical narrative that shaped the course of the continent. Understanding the historical context in which these conquests took place is crucial to appreciating their long-term effects on African societies. The Islamic conquests in Africa were marked by a complex interplay of political, economic, and social factors. They were not just military campaigns but also involved the spread of Islam and the establishment of new political and administrative structures. The conquests brought about significant changes in the political landscape of Africa, creating new power dynamics and reshaping existing social hierarchies. One key aspect of the conquests is the role of local populations in both resisting and accommodating the Islamic invaders. While some communities fiercely resisted the spread of Islam, others saw the potential benefits of aligning with the new ruling elite. This diversity of responses highlights the complexity of the conquests and their impact on different societies across Africa. Furthermore, the Islamic conquests need to be viewed in a broader historical context that includes other imperial expansions throughout history. Comparing the Islamic conquests with other conquests, such as the Roman or Mongol empires, allows us to gain a more nuanced understanding of the dynamics of conquest and the ways in which empires rise and fall. By examining the historical perspectives on the Islamic conquests in Africa, we can appreciate the lasting legacy of these events on the continent. The conquests not only introduced Islam to Africa but also paved the way for cultural exchange, economic development, and political transformation. While they were marked by resistance and conflict, the conquests also laid the foundation for the diverse and dynamic societies that characterize Africa today.

COMPARATIVE ANALYSIS WITH OTHER IMPERIAL EXPANSIONS

The Islamic Conquests in Africa, with their unique blend of religious zeal, military strategy, and cultural diffusion, stand out in the annals of history as a remarkable imperial expansion. To understand the significance and impact of these conquests, it is essential to compare them with other imperial expansions that occurred around the same time or in different regions of the world. One of the key differences between the Islamic Conquests in Africa and other imperial expansions lies in the religious motivation behind the conquests. While many empires sought to expand their territories for economic gain or strategic advantage, the Islamic Conquests were driven by a fervent belief in spreading the message of Islam. This religious zeal not only fueled the rapid expansion of Muslim rule in Africa but also led to the widespread conversion of local populations to Islam. Another significant aspect of the Islamic Conquests is their relatively tolerant approach to governance and administration compared to other imperial powers of the time. The Muslim rulers often allowed local customs and traditions to continue, provided that they did not contradict Islamic law. This flexibility and adaptability helped in the assimilation of diverse African cultures into the expanding Islamic empire. In contrast to the exploitative nature of many imperial expansions, the Islamic Conquests in Africa brought about cultural exchange and mutual enrichment. Through trade, intellectual exchange, and the spread of Islamic scholarship, the Muslim rulers facilitated the development of a vibrant multicultural society in Africa. This stands in stark contrast to the destructive and divisive impact of many other imperial powers that sought to impose their own culture and values on conquered territories. Overall, the Islamic Conquests in Africa offer a unique case study for understanding the dynamics of imperial expansion and its long-term repercussions. By comparing and contrasting these conquests with other imperial expansions, we can gain valuable insights into the complex interplay of religion, culture, and power in shaping the course of history.

LONG-TERM LEGACY OF THE ISLAMIC CONQUESTS IN AFRICA

The long-term legacy of the Islamic conquests in Africa is profound and continues to shape the continent's history and identity to this day. One of the enduring impacts of these conquests is the cultural and intellectual exchange that took place between Arab and African societies. This exchange led to the spread of Islamic knowledge, scholarship, and art across the continent, contributing to the development of vibrant and diverse cultural traditions. Furthermore, the Islamic conquests introduced new systems of governance and administration in Africa, laying the foundation for future political structures in many regions. The establishment of Islamic law and institutions helped to create a sense of unity and cohesion among diverse communities, while also facilitating trade and commerce along trans-Saharan routes. The economic consequences of the Islamic conquests were also significant, as they facilitated the exchange of goods, ideas, and technologies between Africa and the wider Islamic world. This trade network fostered economic growth and prosperity in many regions, leading to the rise of prosperous urban centers and commercial hubs. Moreover, the Islamic conquests had a lasting impact on the religious landscape of Africa, as Islam gradually became a dominant faith in many parts of the continent. This religious transformation not only influenced spiritual beliefs and practices but also shaped social norms, values, and customs in African societies. Despite these positive legacies, the Islamic conquests also sparked resistance and revolts among indigenous African populations who resisted the imposition of foreign rule. These conflicts left a lasting legacy of tensions and conflicts that continue to shape intercommunity relations in Africa today. In conclusion, the long-term legacy of the Islamic conquests in Africa is a complex tapestry of cultural exchange, political transformation, economic development, and religious change. By understanding and appreciating these legacies, we can gain a deeper insight into the historical forces that have shaped the continent and its people over the centuries.

CONTEMPORARY RELEVANCE AND LESSONS LEARNED

The Islamic conquests in Africa have had a lasting impact on the continent, shaping its history and culture in profound ways. Today, the legacy of these conquests continues to be felt, both in Africa and beyond. One of the key lessons learned from the Islamic conquests is the importance of tolerance and coexistence among diverse religious and cultural groups. The ability of Islamic societies to integrate and assimilate different traditions and beliefs has been a driving force behind their longevity and resilience. Additionally, the economic and technological advancements brought about by the Islamic conquests serve as a reminder of the benefits of cross-cultural exchange and collaboration. As we navigate an increasingly interconnected world, the lessons of the Islamic conquests in

Africa offer valuable insights into how different societies can peacefully coexist and thrive together.

www.ingramcontent.com/pod-product-compliance
Lightning Source LLC
Chambersburg PA
CBHW052144070526
44585CB00017B/1963